Running with God

*A discipleship guide to grow in faith and
experience the power and love of God*

Liz Linssen

Also by this author:

10 Steps to Knowing God:
A discipleship guide to developing an
intimate relationship with God for small
groups and personal devotions

10 Steps to Knowing God iPhone app (free)

Contents

· · · · · · · · · · · · ·

Contents

Acknowledgements

I sincerely appreciate all the hard effort and many hours my editor Mike Mack poured into these pages. Thank you too Charse for your time and valued editorial advice.

Introduction

Spend your time and energy in training yourself for spiritual fitness. Physical exercise has some value, but spiritual exercise is much more important, for it promises a reward in both this life and the next.
—1 Timothy 4:7–8, NLT

Is something missing in your spiritual life? Do you ever feel like you're spiritually driving around with the parking brake on? If your answer is yes to these questions and you've been a follower of Jesus Christ for a number of years, then this book is for you. But be cautioned, for as you go through this book you will experience God challenging you to a deeper faith and gently putting His finger on those areas of your life that need some loving attention. You cannot read and apply the teaching of this book and not be challenged.

Running with God is designed to strengthen you in your faith experience and take you to the next level in your spiritual maturity. It will provide you with

- knowledge of how to experience and encounter God in real and wondrous ways

---

- a training program to help you become more disciplined and mature in your relationship with God
- testimonies of individuals who have experienced God moving in their lives
- practical and biblical insight to help you overcome the hindrances that are holding you back from growing spiritually
- confidence in knowing God and the ability to understand His will in everyday situations

This book follows my earlier book, *10 Steps to Knowing God,* in which I talked about what it means to know God and the fundamentals of how to develop a real relationship with Him. *Running with God* has been written to take you a step further into spiritual maturity, teaching you the keys to growing in your faith and dealing with hindrances that might be holding you back. If you believe God is calling you to a greater faith and experience of Him but are not sure how to find it, then keep reading.

I've written this book from the viewpoint of my experiences: East and West. By that I mean that although I'm from the United Kingdom and have been working with many North Americans and American Christian resources in my ministry, my experience of living in Asia for eleven years has given me interesting insights into the kind of Christian faith experience God wants for us. For instance, when Christians pray in South Korea, they raise their voices together in unison. It's a beautiful experience and so powerful to see hundreds and thousands praying at the same time. When believers are sick in China, they pray in expectation until the person is healed. When individuals come to faith in Christ in the Middle East, they do so with the understanding it could cost them their lives.

Although we have a rich heritage of Christianity in the West, with its wonderful resources and church buildings, we lack something believers on the other side of the world have: spiritual vitality and power. *Running with God* is an attempt to bring these two influences together and share with you the best of both worlds in an entirely Biblical context.

There exists today an army of God's people who need to relearn the principles of spiritual growth, how to live by faith, how to read and apply the Bible, how to be led by the Holy Spirit, and how to engage in God's work and miracles among us today. Only when we learn and live out these principles can we live the kind of Spirit- and faith-filled life God desires for us, thus becoming effective disciples and in turn, witnesses of God. After all, we can only be witnesses of God to the degree we've encountered Him.

Using the analogy of sports, this book will teach you how to really know and encounter God, develop your faith, and be led by His Spirit. I pray God will use this book to pour His living water into your Christian experience so your relationship with Him becomes alive, just as you read about in Scripture.

Running with God has been written to enable you to learn how to know God in a real way. Being a Christian is not merely about attending church services and doing what's expected of you; it's about learning how to enter into the fulfillment of His wonderful promises and purpose for your life, receiving from God all He wants to give you, and running your race well. God is awakening a generation of discouraged and immobilized believers to the kind of life the Bible promises. The question is, do you want to be part of it? If you do and are ready to begin this exciting journey together, let's mount the starting blocks!

PART ONE

ON YOUR MARKS

Chapter 1

RACE PREPARATION

*Therefore I tell you, whatever you ask for
in prayer, believe that you have received
it, and it will be yours.*
—Mark 11:24

I have learned by experience that a direct connection exists
between what we do by faith in the everyday, practical
realm and what happens in the spiritual.

Recently, my husband was planning a business trip to
Australia for a few weeks, so he invited me along with him.
It was to be a trip of a lifetime, and to say I was excited
about visiting this amazing country would be an understate-
ment. A few days before we left, I spoke at a Bible study for
mother and toddlers and later that afternoon I found myself
coming down with a sickness. Being around lots of babies,
I guess that was bound to happen. Thankfully, I recovered
somewhat before leaving for Australia.

The morning after arriving in Sydney, I decided to go
to the gym. Bad idea. My sickness returned and I spent the
rest of the week in our rented apartment trying to recover

(note to self: don't go to the gym while suffering jetlag). I took big doses of vitamin C and rested for the remainder of the week, hoping I'd be better by the weekend. By the time the weekend arrived, I was worse. When Sunday rolled around, I'd had enough. This trip of a lifetime, with all the glorious sunshine teasing me outside, wasn't working out as I expected.

That morning a realization began to dawn on me: even though I had been praying for healing, I hadn't actually backed up my prayers with any real faith. Instead, I was doing the very opposite: protecting my sickness by taking medicine and hiding in my apartment. I recognized I needed to change how I was handling this and so I decided to start engaging my faith and believe God for healing.

Although I had originally intended to stay indoors another day, I told my husband I was going to act as if I had been healed (after all that's the spiritual principle Jesus taught us in Mark 11:24, to believe we have received what we ask for in prayer and *then* it will be ours). So I planned a full day of church and tourist activities. From the moment I informed my husband Will of my decision and began getting ready, I started to get better. By the time I left the apartment about an hour later, my head and sinuses had cleared, my sore throat had completely disappeared, and my strength returned. We had a great day and rest of the week together.

I know it's just a small example, but it's illustrative of one great Scriptural truth: *God's power is released when we operate in faith.* In other words, what actions we take by faith in the physical realm enables God's power to be released into our lives from the spiritual. This reality is seen throughout Scripture. For instance:

- When the Israelites were in the desert and found the water was bitter, God showed Moses a piece of wood to throw into the water, which in turn became sweet and drinkable (Exodus 15).
- When the Israelites were fighting the Amalekites, as long as Moses lifted up his hands the Israelites were winning. When he lowered his hands, they were losing (Exodus 17).
- When the men of a city complained to Elisha that the water was bad, the prophet threw salt into the spring and the Lord permanently healed the water (2 Kings 2).
- When Naaman obeyed Elijah and dipped into the Jordan River seven times to be healed of his leprosy, God healed his skin, which then became like that of a young boy (2 Kings 5).
- When Elisha needed to retrieve a lost ax head, he cut a stick of wood and threw it into the water where it was lost and the ax head reappeared (2 Kings 6).
- When Isaiah told King Hezekiah he was going to die, he cried out to God in prayer and God promised he would heal him and add fifteen years to his life. Then Isaiah asked that a poultice of figs be placed on Hezekiah's boil and he was healed (Isaiah 38).
- When people received healing from Jesus in the New Testament, the healing often followed an act of faith (the lame man, woman suffering from

bleeding, Jesus placing mud on a blind man's eyes, and so on).

For a long time whenever I read such passages as these I struggled to understand what the relevance of these acts were. I mean, why did Hezekiah need a poultice of figs applied to his boil if God already promised to heal him? What difference did a piece of wood or bowl of salt make to the pH balance of water? And why did Naaman need to dip in the Jordan River seven times? I've actually seen how green and murky it is and can't see how dipping in that would restore anything. Thankfully God in His grace answered my prayer of curiosity: those physical acts simply represented in faith what the person needed and God's power was released because of their active faith.

There is a relationship between what we do by faith in the practical realm and what happens in the spiritual.

To separate our physical lives from our spiritual lives is a great mistake. If we want to grow in faith, see God's healing, receive victory in life's battles, receive God's provision, see our circumstances change, or be strengthened, then we need to move and operate in faith, which releases God's power in the heavenly realms. Faith is more than just a passive belief. We need to take steps of faith and live like we really believe God's promises. If we believe, then as Jesus promised, we will see the glory of God (John 11:40).

ATHLETES FOR GOD

If anyone competes as an athlete, he does not receive the victor's crown unless he competes according to the rules.
—2 Timothy 2:5

Do you remember when you first came to know God, and what that felt like? I recall clearly when I first became a Christian and started reading the Bible, how God's Word seemed to jump out at me. I soaked in the verses I read, taking them at face value and completely to heart. God answers prayer? Nothing is impossible? God will meet our needs? Wow! *Why hadn't I heard about this amazing God earlier?* I wondered.

Before long I realized not everyone in my new church had this childlike opinion of His Word and how easy it was to settle into a kind of "Christianese" lifestyle—attending church, paying tithes, going on mission trips—yet not really knowing and experiencing the power and love of God in everyday life.

I decided I didn't want that kind of Christian life. I had grown up in a nonreligious family and had seen clearly what living according to the world was like. I was hungry for more and wanted to believe everything the Bible taught. I longed to see God fulfill His promises: heal the sick, provide for our needs, guide us, and even raise the dead. Why not? A lukewarm faith experience wasn't for me. I wanted and still want the real thing.

The fact that you are reading these pages shows you are hungry for a real faith experience too. I wonder how many people reading this book have dreamed about seeing God accomplish something great in their lives, but have been put off from pursuing that because it just seems impossible and nobody else seems to think like that. Yet as we know in our heads, doing the impossible is God's specialty.

As we begin this journey together then, I want you to ask yourself a couple important questions: What kind of Christian life do you really want? Are you willing to really believe God's promises in His Word?

Asking yourself these questions will provide direction as you go through this book. After all, you get what you seek after and you reap what you sow. So, what do you really desire to see in your relationship with God? Take a pen and write some initial thoughts here:

_____

_____

God already knows what He desires to do for you. As Jesus Christ Himself declared, He came to give us life and life to the full (John 10:10). I'm not talking about the quality of life Hollywood or *Hello!* magazine portray, but the Biblical and supernatural kind that experiences answers to prayer, God's power in times of weakness, guidance when confused, and miraculous provision when in need. Beloved, we're talking about raising our expectations of God, just as I shared in my opening testimony. Perhaps this kind of Christian life seems like a far-off reality, but it doesn't have to be.

Please don't misunderstand my intentions. This book is not full of what I call fluffy teaching. I'm not into name-it-and-claim-it, or how-did-you-get-that-from-this-verse kind of creative schooling. This book is practical, yet spiritual and completely Biblical. It's for people who seriously want to live the kind of Christian life the Bible teaches, a real and personal journey between you and your heavenly Father. God wants you to grow in confidence of His ways, Word, and character. He wants you to learn how to flex your muscles, spiritually speaking, because His plan for you is that you become a mighty man or woman of God who brings Him glory and that you ultimately receive the crown of eternal life.

Toward our lofty goals, I am going to utilize the analogy of an athlete, looking at what we can glean from the world of sports. This is not a new idea at all. Indeed, as you will quickly come to realize, the Bible is full of such analogies. I believe there is much we can learn from the practical world of sports that can help us foster and nurture our spiritual walk. Without a doubt, the two are connected.

Becoming a Spiritual Athlete

> *Train yourself to be godly. For physical training is of some value, but godliness has value for all things, holding promise for both the present life and the life to come.*
> —1 Timothy 4:7–8

In these two verses the apostle Paul used a form of the verb *gymnazo* from the original Greek two times. It's easy to see from this word where we got the word for "gymnasium" in

English, and Paul is using it here in the context of how to live and invest into our lives for God. These verses teach us that we need to visit the gym spiritually. That is, we need to invest in spiritual exercise and discipline if we want to grow in God. Spiritual maturity is simply not going to happen by itself. You need to learn how to train to become an athlete for God.

Referring to his own walk with God, Paul at times referred to the discipline of sports, which proved helpful for him and those he taught to understand how to grow and mature spiritually. Consider the following passage:

> Do you not know that in a race all the runners run, but only one gets the prize? Run in such a way as to get the prize. Everyone who competes in the games goes into strict training. They do it to get a crown that will not last; but we do it to get a crown that will last forever. Therefore I do not run like a man running aimlessly; I do not fight like a man beating the air (1 Corinthians 9:24–26).

We can all appreciate how much dedication and devotion it takes to become a successful athlete. All athletes, whatever sport they play, need to pay careful attention to and invest their time and energy into various key areas to improve and ultimately achieve the purpose of all their hard work. Such areas include strength training, nutrition, proper recovery, discipline, and the like. Imagine how a runner or cyclist would perform if he didn't work out to increase his muscular strength or if he didn't eat the right foods.

He certainly wouldn't get very far and couldn't realistically expect to finish his race. The reason why athletes invest in these various areas is because they desire to win a prize. They desire to excel and accomplish success within their given sport.

As 1 Corinthians 9 infers, we need to give careful thought and effort as athletes for God. For example, if we fail to nourish ourselves spiritually or live whatever lifestyle we please, we will not get very far in our Christian journey. As Paul put it, we don't just run aimlessly or foolishly beat the air. Rather, as the New Testament explains, we are spiritual athletes and consequently need to train ourselves to run our race with aim and intention. And as with every sport, this requires discipline.

Perhaps you're inwardly squirming in your chair at the sight of the word *discipline*. But let's be honest with ourselves; isn't it true that everything we hope to accomplish in life requires discipline and effort, whether it's a promotion at work, good relationships, or a healthy diet? Why should it be any different in our journey with God? Why should we expect a strong relationship with and experience of God in our lives if we invest so little? Friend, what we do in the physical realm impacts what happens in the spiritual. The two are connected and God's power is released through our acts of faith. Therefore, whatever you invest into your relationship with God, God will use to grow an abundant spiritual harvest.

Don't misunderstand me. I'm *not* preaching works as the route to spiritual strength and salvation. But I am saying that spiritual growth and maturity will not just happen by itself. If you want to become spiritually fit and strong, running your race well and persevering to the end, you need directed and focused effort and exercise. Why else would the New Testament writers use such an analogy?

Running for a Prize

Perhaps at this point you're asking yourself, why do I need to become a spiritual athlete? Why bother? Excellent question. Honestly, you don't. You can put this book down right now and continue to live your Christian life as you always have. You can choose to walk away from what I'm talking about and not exert yourself any further.

However, if you're hungry for more of God, if you want to really grow in faith and His power, then this is one way to encourage that to happen. Spiritual growth doesn't happen through good intentions alone. In fact, nothing happens through good intentions. It's only when intentions are mixed with effort that good results happen. So like I said, it's your choice. No one is forcing this upon you. It's simply an invitation to become fit spiritually and learn how to run an exciting race with God.

If you courageously choose to come along on this adventure, then it is indeed a worthwhile exercise to understand *why* you are about to do this. So here's a small summary of some wonderful and worthwhile goals:

- to know God and His power and love more
- to live God's amazing purposes in your life
- to experience what it really means to live by faith
- to receive eternal life

Every athlete who runs in a race has a goal. There is always a prize. Similarly, we too run our race for a prize, a reward—two rewards in fact, as we read in 1 Timothy 4 earlier: "holding promise for both the *present life* and the *life to come*." The promise is not just about eternity: there are rewards in the present life *and* in the life to come. Reward for the present life would have been enough to get me off my sofa, but eternal life too? Awesome.

Yes, God promises us a far greater prize: a crown that will last forever. We discipline ourselves and learn how to become fit and healthy athletes that we might run our race well and finally win our ultimate prize of salvation. This salvation is not given to the disqualified. Nor is it given to the careless or disobedient. It is only given to those who remain in Christ to the end. Those who win the prize of eternal life are those who have successfully worked out their salvation and have persevered:

> He who stands firm to the end will be saved (Matthew 24:13).

> We want each of you to show this same diligence to the very end, in order to make your hope sure. We do not want you to become lazy, but to imitate those who through faith and patience inherit what has been promised (Hebrews 6:11–12).

Running for Your Life

Sadly, too many people do not know how to run their race well and thus are not finishing; too many are giving up and turning their backs on God when the trials and tests of life hit. This breaks God's heart. It happens simply because they do not understand God's will and love for them. Many fall into the mistaken thinking that God is the author of the evil in their lives and so they turn away from Him. Dear friend, I do not want you to go down that same path. Instead, decide today to grow in your relationship with God and in your understanding of His will and love for you. Determine to seek God through the troubles that come your way and know His faithfulness for you through them.

Let us then fix our eyes on our prize: reward in this present life and eternal life to come. This is why we run, why we will learn how to train and discipline ourselves: we are running for our very lives. How we live matters, for as Scripture clearly teaches, the life God wants us to live will not just happen automatically:

> For this very reason, make every effort to add to your faith, goodness; and to goodness, knowledge; and to knowledge, self-control; and to self-control, perseverance; and to perseverance, godliness; and to godliness, brotherly kindness; and to brotherly kindness, love. ... Therefore, my brothers, be all the more eager to make your calling and election sure. For if you do these things, you will never fall, and you will receive a rich welcome into the eternal kingdom of our Lord and Savior Jesus Christ (2 Peter 1:5–7, 10–11).

Decision Time

Friend, are you willing to sow and invest into your relationship with God? Are you ready to become a fit and strong athlete for God? Please pause and take a few moments to decide whether you are really willing to fully commit to the training program. All athletes who desire to succeed in their sport begin with this same decision of commitment: to give it their best, or not. You need to do the same. Internationally acclaimed sport psychologist Terry Orlick highlights the importance and power of decisions:

> Virtually everything that you do or do not do in your life is ruled by the choices that you make. You can choose to excel or choose not to excel. You can choose to bring focus and quality to what you do or choose not to. ... You can choose to embrace your dreams and go after them or let them drift away without really trying. These are your choices, and your choices direct the quality of your performance and the joyfulness of your life. You decide.[1]

According to Orlick, if athletes are going to truly achieve excellence, if they are going to realize their dreams, they must begin by making that all-important decision to give it their best. If athletes who run for mere accolades and medals understand the importance of giving their very best, how much more should we? God is not merely looking for the leftovers of our time and energy after we've spent it on everything else. Many of us are prepared to give our best to our job, our family, or those other areas that are important to us. The question is, are you now ready to give your best to God?

1. Read 2 Timothy 2:5. According to this verse, how does an athlete receive the victor's crown?

    _____

    _____

2. Now read verse 6. What does the hardworking farmer receive?

    _____

    _____

3. Read 2 Corinthians 9:6. How does this harvest principle relate to your relationship with God?

    _____

    _____

PRAYER OF COMMITMENT

Dear Father God,

I thank You, Lord, for calling me to the path of discipleship and spiritual maturity, the greatest calling in my life. I decide

*here and now that I truly want to be a strong athlete and com-
mit to maturing in my relationship with You.*

*God, I don't expect this to be easy, and I know I won't
get it perfect, but I ask You to help me through this process.
Strengthen me, Lord, and encourage me in my faith. Bring others to encourage me and help me. You are the One who makes
all things grow, and so I ask You to enable me to grow in You,
as You desire.*

*I fully commit and surrender to You. In the name of Jesus
Christ I pray, amen.*

HINDRANCES HAMPER

*Therefore, since we are surrounded by such a great
cloud of witnesses, let us throw off everything that
hinders and the sin that so easily entangles, and let us
run with perseverance the race marked out for us.*
—Hebrews 12:1

Well done! The fact that you are reading this section means
you have decided to commit to this journey of spiritual
maturity. What follows in this chapter might not be the
easiest teaching to swallow, but it is essential for spiritual
growth. Compare this to a visit to your dentist if you like,
something that might not be the most pleasant of experiences, but beneficial to your overall health. So let's examine
some "spiritual cavities," those issues or hindrances that
hold you back from going deeper with God.

Hindrances Impede

In the world of sports, athletes face occasional unwanted upsets or setbacks in their training or performance. To compete, these athletes must address and deal with the issue, whether it's a weak muscle, injury, external stress, poor practice style, or something else. They know that to ignore it would be foolish and detrimental to their future success.

The same is true for us. Certain areas of some of our lives have become obstacles and barriers to our spiritual growth. Imagine a hurdler trying to clear the hurdles with weights around his ankles, or an ice skater gliding around a rink full of bricks or potholes. Not only would it be dangerous, but it would be impossible to perform well. The same is true in the spiritual realm: *Hindrances have the power to prevent you from maturity and living the full life Jesus promises.* Let me share one true case to exemplify what I mean.

I have a friend whom I'll call John. John sincerely desires to grow spiritually in his relationship with God. He goes to church, serves faithfully, and enjoys fellowship with other believers. Yet he is frustrated because he is not growing in his faith as he should be, and it's been like this for many years.

A few months ago, he shared with me one area in which he has been struggling for a long time: finances. He simply can't get his finances sorted out and save for his future. He went on to mention how he knows he should be tithing, but because he is struggling to manage his finances and get himself out of debt, he chooses not to. He understands this is an area where God wants him to trust and obey Him, but he's too afraid to give the reins to God. But that's not the only problem.

Because of his poor money management, he doesn't feel he can get married and provide for a family even though this is something he really longs to do. Can you see what is happening here? Because he hasn't surrendered this area of finances to God and hasn't learned how to walk in faith and obedience in this area, it's not only hampering his spiritual growth, in turn it's affecting his confidence in getting married. If only he took a step of faith and trusted God, not only would he see God honor his obedience and provide for him, but also his faith would grow, which in turn would give him the confidence to get married. What he's doing (or not doing) spiritually is affecting him practically. It's a hindrance.

Can you see how one seemingly small area of disobedience can have a much larger impact? It just takes one hindrance to stunt our growth and progress in God and impact our life as a whole.

We don't often realize the power of hindrances to hold us back from developing our relationship with God. We think one little area of disobedience doesn't matter much, that our unwillingness to trust God is no big deal. But it is. It only takes one hindrance to affect everything else and stop you from making progress spiritually.

For that reason, before we look at the principles of maturity, first come before God in prayer and ask Him to show you whether there is any hindrance in your life. You can only truly learn how to run with God if you have freed yourself from anything that might be holding you back. Pray and ask God to bring to mind whether there is something getting in the way of your progress. You may wish to use the prayer I've provided at the end of this section. Don't be afraid of coming to God about this. Your heavenly Father is very loving and by His Spirit will gently bring to mind if there is anything you need to deal with. Whatever comes to mind, take it seriously and be willing to deal with it. If it is something you need to repent of, do that and experience God's love and release in that area. If it is something practical you need to change or a relationship you need to address, ask for God's help, strength, and guidance. Whatever the hindrance may be, let God lovingly help you remove that shackle.

4. What are some common obstacles that often prevent believers from becoming spiritually fit?

_____

_____

5. Read Galatians 5:7. Write it out here:

_____

_____

Hindrances Distract

As the writer states in Hebrews 12:1, these believers had been running a good race previously but were no longer doing so. In their particular situation, it was an individual who was throwing them into confusion and causing them to stumble. Don't underestimate the power of hindrances, whatever form they take. Read what J. Oswald Sanders writes on this subject:

> There is an interesting Greek story of Atalanta and Hippomenes. The fleet-footed Atalanta challenged any young man to a race. The reward of victory would be her hand in marriage. The penalty of defeat would be death. ... Hippomenes accepted her challenge, but before setting out on the race, he secreted on his person three golden apples. When the race began, Atalanta easily outstripped him. He took out a golden apple and rolled it in front of her. The glitter of the gold caught her eye, and as she stopped to pick it up, he shot past her. She quickly recovered and again outdistanced him. Another golden apple rolled across her track, and again she stopped to pick it up, allowing Hippomenes again to sweep past her. The goal was near and he was ahead, but once more she overtook him. Seizing his last chance, he rolled the third apple, and while Atalanta wavered, Hippomenes reached the tape. They were married and lived happily ever after!

Our wily adversary is adept in deploying his golden apples. He does not observe the rules of the game, and he will use every subtlety to prevent our winning the prize. But Paul had every reason to claim, "We are not unaware of his schemes" (2 Corinthians 2:11). Not all of us are able to make a similar assertion.

Too many are spiritual illiterates when it comes to discerning and anticipating his subtleties.[2]

Just one obstacle has the power to distract your focus from running your race. The point is, hindrances are effective and Satan loves to use them, often convincing us it's OK to put off dealing with such things. Don't be fooled. As the writer of Hebrews 12:1 exhorts us, "throw off everything that hinders and the sin that so easily entangles." Don't allow your adversary to distract or sidetrack you with his "golden apples."

Father God,

I know I have not been running with You as I should have been and have allowed other things to distract and hinder me from following You. God, I'm so sorry about that.

Heavenly Father, please reveal to me now by Your Spirit whether there is anything or anyone in my life that is holding me back from truly running after You.

Today I decide before You to stop this downward path. Please forgive me for any sin and help me grow again in You. I here and now surrender all my life to You afresh and choose to obey You in this area, _____, which I know You are pointing out to me.

Help me to be able to make the changes I need to make and let me see You powerfully at work in my life. Make me a strong athlete and follower.

In the name of Jesus Christ I pray, amen.

FREE FROM FOOTHOLDS

Do not give the devil a foothold.
—Ephesians 4:27

Previously we looked at how hindrances have the ability to block our growth and maturity as followers of Christ. We saw how one simple area of disobedience can affect not only our relationship with God, but other areas of our lives as well. Next I want us to go a bit deeper into this topic of things that hinder God's purposes in our lives and look at footholds in the spiritual realm. By "footholds," I mean ways the devil finds entrance into areas of our lives to cause us trouble.

While hindrances can prevent and hamper spiritual growth, footholds go a step further. When we willfully disobey God in some particular area of our lives for a lengthy period of time without repenting, we provide a place for the devil to oppress us in some way. It's a spiritual reality that we need to be aware of because footholds both hinder and give authority to the enemy to do his evil work.

A young woman whom I'll call Amy experienced this. Amy was a lovely Christian woman in her twenties who was serving at our church. She had been growing in God the previous few years, and had even experienced a miraculous physical healing while in the hospital. Seeing God powerfully healing her bolstered her faith.

Amy had been praying for a husband and one man came into her life and asked her to marry him. But he was a nonbeliever and so, being her pastor, I felt I needed to lovingly and gently explain to her what the Bible says about marrying nonbelievers. I explained what God's will, as the Bible teaches it, is in this area as well as some of the practical difficulties she might encounter if she did go ahead and marry her unbelieving suitor. I explained the challenges she would face with raising her children in the ways of the Lord, differences in values, possible pressure to reduce her church attendance, potential jealously from her husband because of her love for God, and so forth.

As our talk progressed, she mentioned another man who had shown interest in marrying her, and that he was actually a Christian pastor. However, as we talked, it was clear she had no real interest in him. I exhorted her to carefully consider her decision and encouraged her to obey God and not marry a nonbeliever as she would not only be disobeying God, but she would probably end up suffering great stress in the long run.

Eventually she decided to marry the nonbeliever. Because of her decision, many of the other unmarried women in our church circle were surprised and began to question their own convictions on marriage.

About a year after her marriage, we met and talked. She told me how after she married, her sickness had returned and also how she was struggling with her mother-in-law, who of course, was not a believer either and had a different set of values and expectations from her. She knew God loved her but, because of her decision, she was beginning to experience the practical and spiritual consequences. You see, through her disobedience to God she had stepped out of His protection and provision and in turn gave the enemy an entranceway into her life to trouble her, which is why her sickness returned.

Many believers in churches wonder why they are not maturing in their faith. Yet when pressed, some will readily admit they know of areas in their lives in which they are not obeying God, areas they know God has spoken to them about in the past, but which they have not taken seriously. Dear friend, don't be deceived. That area of disobedience may be whole reason you are not maturing in your faith. Disobedience not only has the power to hold us back from going deeper in our relationship with God, it also opens up a way for the enemy to come against us. That is, we give the enemy a foothold in our lives.

As the surrounding verses of Ephesians 4:27 make clear, it is sin that gives the devil a foothold, while walking in righteousness and holiness will prevent that from happening. This same word translated "foothold" in Ephesians 4:27 is the same word translated as "place" in Matthew 12:43: "When an evil spirit comes out of a man, it goes through arid *places* seeking rest and does not find it."

When we give the devil a foothold into our lives through sin, we are giving him a place, an entranceway, to start bothering us with his works, which are not hard to discern. They include fear, anxiety, confusion, oppression, or lack of peace. It is only when we repent that this foothold, or place, is given back over to God's influence and protection. Isaiah 54:17 says, "'No weapon forged against you will prevail, and you will refute every tongue that accuses you. This is the heritage of the servants of the Lord, and this is their vindication from me,' declares the Lord." As Cindy Jacobs aptly puts it,

> Note that this Scripture does not say that the weapon will not be formed or sent, but that it will not prosper. We need to stay pure and holy before the Lord, walking in forgiveness, so that we will not have any holes in our armor for the evil one to attack."[3]

If we do not walk in obedience to God but rather willfully compromise, then we're walking a dangerous path and are giving the devil a foothold into our lives. That happens because, through our sin, he has every spiritually legal right to do so. That essentially is what happened to Adam and Eve in the Garden of Eden. Through their sin and willful disobedience, they gave the enemy an entranceway for his evil work not only into their own lives, but into the world as a whole. John Bevere wrote on this subject,

> Under the divine law of God, our enemy is restricted to the realm of darkness. As believers, we are delivered from these powers of darkness. But if this door is opened, Satan and his cohorts are granted legal entrance. Their objective: to control areas of our lives. This always results in theft, destruction, and a loss of freedom. It can even mean our lives.[4]

Even Jesus talked about this spiritual reality: "I will not speak with you much longer for the prince of this world is coming. He has no hold on me" (John 14:30). The *English*

Standard Version translates the sentence as: "he has no claim on me." When Jesus was tempted in the desert for those forty days, He was extremely hungry and in great need. He could have rebelled against God the Father, turning His back on dependency on Him and done things His own way. But He didn't. He submitted Himself to God the Father and obeyed Him completely, resisting the temptations of the devil to compromise. As a result of His obedience and submission, Satan had no access or entrance into any area of His life. As Jesus put it, Satan had no hold on Him.

Don't be fooled. Selective or delayed obedience is disobedience: "Anyone, then, who knows the good he ought to do and doesn't do it, sins" (James 4:17). There is no such thing as an obedient Christian who compromises. God is looking for our wholehearted obedience and submission to His will in our lives. Anything else is rebellion, and you know how God feels about that:

> Does the Lord delight in burnt offerings and sacrifices as much as in obeying the voice of the Lord? To obey is better than sacrifice, and to heed is better than the fat of rams. For rebellion is like the sin of divination, and arrogance like the evil of idolatry (1 Samuel 15:22–23).

It doesn't matter how many church services we attend, how much money we give to the Lord, or what good works we do, if we are walking in disobedience to God in other areas, we stunt our growth and give the enemy a foothold into our lives. The good news is that the power of that foothold can be broken. We can close any entranceway through our genuine repentance and surrender. I love the promise of James 4:7: "Submit yourselves, then, to God. Resist the devil, and he will flee from you."

Satan cannot succeed in the face of an obedient follower. Obedience is more powerful than you realize. As you submit yourself to God's will and righteous ways, and as you resist the enemy, Satan will flee. Not just walk away; he will flee! That's a promise.

However, if we walk in disobedience, a foothold can develop over time into something bigger, a stronghold. Please understand I'm *not* talking about possession (as Christians we are filled with God's Spirit), but I'm talking about influence or oppression in a particular area such as addiction, bitterness, anger, or even physical or mental sickness. It's as if we've left a door in our house unlocked and provided the thief with a way to come in and steal our belongings. He can't take possession of the whole house, but he can certainly cause some real trouble.

Maybe there is an area of your life where you recognize the work of the enemy, but perhaps you just don't know how you can overcome that. Beloved, all God is expecting from you is your *willingness*. As you pray and tell God you're willing to change in that particular area, God will set you free. The enemy will immediately lose control and God will take back that area of your life under His loving care and protection.

God desires to set you free and bring you peace. To mature as a disciple of Christ, allow God to set you free from any area of the influence of the enemy. You cannot progress unless you do. Stop now and spend time in prayer. Ask God to show you if there is any area of your life in which the enemy has gained a foothold and repent of that before God. You may wish to use the following prayer.[5]

PRAYER

Father God, I ask You now to show me if there is any area of my life I have not submitted in obedience to You.

God, please forgive me for this sin. My sincere desire is to now obey You in this, so please cleanse me from my sin. I surrender this area of my life to You and Your control. Fill me with Your Holy Spirit I pray, and surround me with Your divine protection.

In Christ's name I pray, amen.

6. Read 2 Corinthians 11:2–4. How would you rephrase these verses into your own words? What are some ways the enemy tries to deceive us?

_____

_____

7. Now read James 1:22–25. According to James, how is it possible that we can deceive ourselves? What is the fruit of the person who obeys God's Word?

_____

_____

8. Is there any known area of compromise in your life? Spend time privately praying about this and surrendering it to God.

EXCUSING EXCUSES

At the time of the banquet he sent his servant to tell those who had been invited, "Come, for everything is now ready." But they all alike began to make excuses.
—Luke 14:17–18

I want to commend you for getting through the last few tough sections. Persevere with me as we go through one final toughie: hiding behind excuses in our walks with God.

Joyce Meyer utilizes a wonderful illustration in this area. She talks about an "excuse bag," something she believes we carry around, filled with excuses we selectively pull out and give to God whenever He asks us to do something either we're afraid of or we just don't want to do. These excuses include:

- I'm not strong enough spiritually.
- I don't know how to do that.
- I have too many personal problems of my own.

- It's too difficult.
- I don't have enough money.
- I'm waiting for God to call me first.
- I'm not ready for that yet.
- I've never done this before.
- I'm too shy and lack confidence.
- I'm afraid.
- I've got too many other commitments.
- My partner isn't a believer yet.
- I'm not married yet.
- I've got to sort out my problems first.

Whether it's a genuine lack of confidence or an old-fashioned lack of obedience, there are many reasons to which we cling that prevent us from progressing and growing in God. Perhaps it was a negative experience years ago that has convinced you God cannot or does not want to use you in some wonderful way. Or maybe it's simply that no one has ever encouraged or affirmed you in what you're good at.

Whatever the rationale, sometimes we can allow these genuine and heartfelt reasons to develop into excuses from running with God. Dear reader, it's time to no longer allow that belief to hold you back from fulfilling God's will and purposes in your life. As so many, including me, have found, God can heal you of any negative experience or pain you have had. He can also help you discover your strengths and spiritual gifts and give you the courage and boldness you need to step out for Him. Whatever may have been genuinely holding you back, God can enable you to overcome. There is no need to allow anything to stop you from becoming an amazing athlete for God. Let's look at one example from the Bible.

When God called Moses, Moses had a serious lack of confidence whether he was the right man for the job. What is interesting is that he hadn't always been that way: "Moses was educated in all the wisdom of the Egyptians and was powerful in speech and action" (Acts 7:22).

Although in his earlier years he had been described as powerful in both how he spoke and what he did, now in his old age he felt very different. So when God called him to become the leader of His people the Israelites, to speak before Pharaoh and lead God's people out of slavery in Egypt, Moses was the last person who wanted the job. Read the conversation between Moses and God in Exodus 3:1–4:17 and answer the following questions:

9. What was the specific task God wanted Moses to do?

_____

_____

10. Why did he think he was the wrong person for the job? How did he view himself?

_____

_____

11. Reread Exodus 4:13. What was Moses' request to God after their lengthy conversation?

_____

_____

Before we accuse Moses of being slow in his obedience, we need to realize that perhaps at times we have been guilty of the exact same excuse: "Oh Lord, I can't do it. Please send someone else." Has God ever asked you to do something, however small or big, and you refused to do it for whatever reason? It may not have been a blatant "No, God, I'm not going to do that!" It may have been a simple case of telling God how inadequate you felt, as Moses did.

You need to understand that there is no reason, other than your willingness, why you cannot do what God wants you to do. Why? Because Scripture teaches us that God can empower us to do His will despite our real, human weaknesses:

> "My grace is sufficient for you, for my power is made perfect in weakness." Therefore I will boast all the more gladly about my weaknesses, so that Christ's power may rest on me. ... For when I am weak, then I am strong (2 Corinthians 12:9, 10).

These words were penned by the apostle Paul yet show how this great man of God also felt moments of weakness. Despite how weak he thought of himself, when he cried out to God in prayer, God showed him that if he chose to depend on Him despite the weaknesses he felt, he would experience the power of God. The same will be true for you.

I vividly remember one simple example of this from my own life. I'd had a busy week and on this particular day had several pastoral appointments that left me drained physically and emotionally. I had one more person to meet before the day was out, but I felt too exhausted to do it. I sat on the sofa and told God how tired I was feeling and how much I needed Him to strengthen me. He brought this verse from 2 Corinthians 12 to mind and in response I told God I believed His promise. With that, I got up from my chair with a determined and faith-filled attitude, and as I did so I literally felt the power of the Holy Spirit surge through my body. In just a moment, I was completely physically revived. I'm not exaggerating. I was amazed and joyfully went to my next appointment greatly encouraged and full of joy.

God means what He says in His Word. God's promises are not hyperbole or given to merely make us feel better. God's Word is truth. As a result, it really doesn't matter how weak or inadequate we feel because, at the end of the day, it is God who enables us to do His will. In fact, we should view our weaknesses as opportunities to see God move and experience His power and glory:

> God chose the foolish things of the world to shame the wise; God chose the weak things of the world to shame the strong. He chose the lowly things of the world and the despised things—and the things that

are not—to nullify the things that are, so that no one may boast before him (1 Corinthians 1:27–29).

All God needs from you is your willing heart of obedience. He will do the rest. There is nothing He cannot enable you to do: "I can do everything through him who gives me strength" (Philippians 4:13).

The Bible is replete with wonderful promises for every individual who is willing to step out and simply take Him at His Word. God doesn't call you to do something for Him because of who you are or your talents but because you are simply willing to take Him at His Word and obey. Are you willing to follow God where He is leading you? If you are, it's time to throw away your excuse bag.

ATHLETIC TRAINING PROGRAM

Let no one despise you for your youth, but set the believers an example in speech, in conduct, in love, in faith, in purity.
—1 Timothy 4:12, ESV

Now that you've spent time working on those issues that can hinder you from growing in God, it's time to climb out of the dentist's chair and focus your attention on the training program that will assist you toward your goal of spiritual maturity.

As with many things in life, such as learning to drive a car, acquiring a new language, or gaining new job skills, an established model of effective learning or a training program has already been laid down by previous teachers to assist the student in his or her endeavor to learn. It is no different in our walk with God.

The Bible reveals instruction already laid down by the great Christian leaders of the New Testament that show us how to live to please God and how to mature as believers in Jesus Christ. These writers offer their lives as examples to follow and imitate as we run this race in today's world. As Paul said, "Follow my example, as I follow the example of Christ" (1 Corinthians 11:1).

To help you become spiritually fit, we are going to use one specific training program, which I have called the "five-fold model," based on the five areas outlined in the opening verse of this section, 1 Timothy 4:12: "Let no one despise you for your youth, but set the believers an example in speech, in conduct, in love, in faith, in purity." In this verse, the writer defines five specific areas in which he desired his student, Timothy, to focus on in order to further grow and mature in his faith: *speech, conduct, love, faith,* and *purity.* To suit our sports paradigm, I have interpreted these five areas into relevant athletic terms: *attitude, strength training, devotion, perseverance,* and *nutrition.* In the following chapters of this book, these five areas will provide the infrastructure of our training program.

As the Biblical writers taught, each of these five areas is important to mature and run our race as fit spiritual athletes. It's not arbitrary that several New Testament writers used the analogy of an athlete and sports when explaining how to become a fit and worthy disciple of Jesus Christ. They understood how becoming spiritually strong requires training and discipline in various areas. Each aspect of training is important and not to be neglected if success is to be attained, whether on the physical field or on God's track.

A year ago I decided it was time to lose those extra kilograms that had been creeping up on me throughout my thirties. Being involved in busy full-time pastoral ministry with no time for fitness had produced the unfit condition in which I found myself. However, I also realized I needed some help. I didn't have a clue about how to get fit and knew nothing about losing weight.

So I decided to embark on a diploma of fitness management. It was a new and different kind of subject for me, but I realized I simply needed to learn the basics and get some encouragement and motivation. So I enrolled with an online college and each month they sent me the lessons, which I read and soaked in. I learned so much and really grew in confidence as I saw the results of my hard work. Little by little over time, the knowledge I gained plus the training and discipline I put in worked together to enable me to lose the extra weight and strengthen my weak muscles. In the same way, to become spiritually fit we need to put in the time and effort *and* grow in knowledge.

Your Training Manual: The Bible

As 2 Timothy 3:16 affirms, instruction and growing in knowledge is profitable, inspiring, and useful, especially when it's in the Word of God: "All Scripture is God-breathed and is useful for teaching, rebuking, correcting and training in righteousness, so that the man of God may be thoroughly equipped for every good work."

12. Read 1 Timothy 4:11–16. What did Paul encourage Timothy to do?

_____

_____

13. What kind of example was Timothy encouraged to become?

_____

_____

Paul encouraged Timothy to set an example to other believers and to be diligent in the disciplines that would produce spiritual progress. In other words, he was giving Timothy good instruction for growing as a Christian leader. Just because Timothy had started well in his faith didn't guarantee he would finish well. In fact, earlier in his letter to Timothy, he mentioned two believers who unfortunately failed to progress and who had in fact abandoned their faith:

> Timothy, my dear son, I give you this instruction in keeping with the prophecies once made about you, so that by following them you may fight the good fight, holding on to the faith and a good conscience. Some have rejected these and so have shipwrecked their faith. Among them are Hymenaeus and Alexander,

whom I have handed over to Satan to be taught not to blaspheme (1 Timothy 1:18–20).

Paul taught Timothy to "[hold] on to the faith" being careful not to turn his back on the growth he had already made in his journey with God and to continue his spiritual maturity. Timothy was blessed to have had a good start in his Christian experience, especially because his family had positively influenced and instructed him in his faith as he grew up (2 Timothy 1:5). Even so, Paul taught him the value of God's Word. Timothy still hadn't "arrived" spiritually speaking and still needed to grow, which would happen through the discipline of reading and application of God's Word. This was key for Timothy's growth, as it is for yours. God's Word is your training manual and will be a central and vital part of our journey together in this book.

Your Personal Coach: The Holy Spirit

You are not alone in your quest to become stronger spiritually. Just as with every professional athlete, you have your own personal Coach, God the Holy Spirit, the third person of the Trinity. As a born-again believer, the Bible explains how you are a temple of the Holy Spirit (1 Corinthians 3:16), the place where God Himself dwells:

> And I will ask the Father, and he will give you another Counselor to be with you forever—the Spirit of truth. The world cannot accept him, because it neither sees him nor knows him. But you know him, for *he*

lives with you and will be in you. ... The Counselor, the Holy Spirit, whom the Father will send in my name, *will teach you all things* and will remind you of everything I have said to you (John 14:16–17, 26, emphasis added).

When God through His Spirit lives in you, you have everything you need to be able to grow and mature. You have the resources of God at your disposal, for God Himself will teach you and give you revelation of His will and character as you ask: "I keep asking that the God of our Lord Jesus Christ, the glorious Father, may give you the Spirit of wisdom and revelation, so that you know him better" (Ephesians 1:17).

God's power lives in you when you are baptized into the Holy Spirit (Acts 19:1–6).[6] Having received His Spirit and power, you have everything you need to be able to grow and mature in Christ. The only thing God requires from you is your willingness to exercise your faith. As you do your part, God will do His. As you put in the time and discipline and follow His leading, God will produce a wonderful harvest of spiritual growth. It's the law of sowing and reaping: you sow your seeds of faith and obedience, and God enables you to reap a spiritual harvest in return.

God the Holy Spirit will teach and guide you, encourage and strengthen you. He will give you the wisdom, understanding, and revelation of His will and purpose for your life that you long for. As you seek, you will find. As you ask, He will answer you (Matthew 7:7–8).

I urge you at the beginning of this training program to learn how to rely on the Holy Spirit to guide you through this process and enable you to grow. Don't make the mistake many believers make by underestimating the role of God the Holy Spirit to lead and guide you. Partner together with your Coach and listen for His voice. Depend on Him and believe God desires to speak to you and help you grow. We will look at the role of the Holy Spirit in more depth later in this book.

As you assume your responsibility of sowing the seeds of spiritual growth into your life, God will do His part and bring a rich harvest of spiritual maturity. May God strengthen and bless you as you invest in your personal training program.

14. Reread 1 Timothy 4:16. Why do you think the writer outlined these five specific areas (given in verse 13)? Why are they important?

_____

_____

15. Now read 2 Timothy 1:7. According to this verse, what has God already given us to enable us to grow in Him?

_____

_____

APPLICATION QUESTIONS

Whether in a small group or alone, read through and prayerfully answer the following questions. Ask the Lord to guide you and speak to your heart.

1. What specific parallels can you see between the world of sport and spiritual health and fitness?

_____

_____

2. What is one area in which you desire to see improvement in your relationship with God?

_____

_____

3. Is there a bad habit that is stunting your spiritual growth? How does God want you to respond?

_____

_____

4. In your opinion, why is wholehearted obedience important? Share any experience that comes to mind.

_____

_____

5. Read 2 Corinthians 9:8. According to this verse, what is God able to make happen for you?

_____

_____

6. Have you experienced God's Spirit speaking to you or guiding you? Share that with a friend.

_____

_____

7. What is one area God has spoken to you about through this chapter? How will you respond to Him?

_____

_____

Chapter 2

ATTITUDE DETERMINES DESTINY

Do you not know that in a race all the runners run, but only one gets the prize? Run in such a way as to get the prize. Everyone who competes in the games goes into strict training. They do it to get a crown that will not last; but we do it to get a crown that will last forever.
—1 Corinthians 9:24–25

At one time in my life I thought I knew why God allows people to experience times of pain. Then I faced the first devastation in my own life. To be sure, pain hurts, but now I know beyond a mere intellectual understanding how God can use it to open my eyes to seek and find the "true God."

My painful experience started when I turned thirty-four. On the face of things, nothing appeared wrong in my life. I held a decent teaching post at a reputable college and things were working out just fine. However, inside I was struggling with my *deep desire to explore a new frontier in my field. Although I was teaching, I wanted to develop a customized English-education program for groups of people in many fields. I saw the potential market, but there was no concept of "customization" in the area at that time and I had no resources to start a business specializing in this.*

I knew my limits. I was far from a business-oriented person and it seemed impossible. Whenever I thought about being a teacher forever, I felt suffocated. As time went by, these feelings of helplessness grew and eventually became intense; I couldn't find any reason for living. You might think, as I once did, that only traumatic events can cause feelings of suicide, but that was not the case for me. I felt like my life was not worth living. Eventually I found myself thinking of death and that there was someone else inside of me.

Thankfully, completely drained, I didn't have the energy to get enough sleeping pills to kill myself, and I realized I needed to talk to someone before I did find a way. That in itself was not an easy thing to do. Before I eventually confided in my pastor, I struggled with the thought that she could do nothing about this, that she could never fully understand my despair since she hadn't been there. As it turned out, she was the one God prepared for me, and through her guidance, God started to heal me. If she had said, "you shouldn't kill yourself. It's against God," I might not have been able to overcome this. Instead she just helped me to get closer to God.

One significant thing God did in my life at this time was to heal me of a terrible allergy I'd suffered with for many years. My diet was so limited that if I happened to eat something unsuitable, painful sores and swellings erupted on most of my body. It was agony. My pastor encouraged me to believe God for healing and strongly urged me to attend a conference that a speaker with a known healing ministry was attending. I was reluctant at first, but after her serious and persuasive words, I eventually went. When I entered the building, before I heard any words from the speaker, I knew God had healed me. He set me free! I was amazed and thrilled at God's love for me.

Through that miracle, plus good teaching through books and overflowing prayers, God changed all my mistaken beliefs about him and made me realize that if I plan and dream about something good, it is by God's power, not mine, that I can truly realize it. God also healed me of my desire to commit suicide and truly set me free.

With this newfound hope and understanding about God, I started my business two years ago. Still I suffer from self-doubts and fear of failure since I know I have a long way to go. The way before me is not paved with gold, but now I am sure that as long as God is with me, even failures can be meaningful. God is a wonderful God who transforms us, inside and out.

Sungjoo

POWER OF THINKING

*You were taught, with regard to your former way of
life, to put off your old self, which is being corrupted
by its deceitful desires; to be made new in the attitudes
of your minds; and to put on the new self, created to
be like God in true righteousness and holiness.*
—Ephesians 4:22–24

How you think and what you believe affects the direction
of your life. Your thoughts are powerful.

In sports, a healthy and positive mental attitude is often
what determines success or failure. For instance, the attitude
an athlete adopts will determine whether he perseveres in the
face of setbacks, whether he accepts responsibility for his own
performance and training, and whether he is goal-focused or
simply blown about by circumstances and emotions. A right
attitude enables athletes to not only enjoy their sport but to
achieve what they had set out to do when they first started.

Similarly, a right and healthy attitude and way of thinking toward God and setbacks we encounter are important
as we run our spiritual race. After all, the condition of our
hearts affects all areas of our lives: the decisions we make,
where we spend our attention and time, how we think
about God and ourselves, whether we are disciplined, how
we treat others, whether we trust God, and so on. Basically,
the thoughts and attitudes of our heart and mind influence
everything. Proverbs 23:7 summarizes it succinctly: "For as
he thinks in his heart, so is he" (*New King James Version*).
I love what Joyce Meyer says about this verse:

This one Scripture alone lets us know how very important it is that we think properly. Thoughts are powerful, and according to the writer of the book of Proverbs, they have creative ability. If our thoughts are going to affect what we become, then it should certainly be a priority that we think right thoughts.[1]

It's true: what we think in our hearts and minds influences the people we become, which is why our attitude is the first element we will look at together in our training program. What people see on the outside directly reveals what is going on inside, for how we think ultimately expresses itself in our words and behavior. Therefore, it's important that we pay attention to how we think, because our thoughts will directly affect our outward, everyday life.

Wrong Thoughts about Yourself

It's sad that so many people are bound up in negative or wrong thinking that holds them back from developing as God desires. Do any of the following statements sound familiar to you?

- God doesn't really love me.
- I've made too many mistakes.
- I have no future.
- I'm unworthy of God's attention.
- God doesn't want to use me.
- I don't have any spiritual gifts.
- I'm not important enough.
- I'm not good enough.

- God is not interested in me.
- My family background is too bad.
- I'm too sinful.
- I don't have enough faith.
- I'm too insignificant.
- I'm too old for God to use me.

These lies do not originate from God but from our adversary, the devil, and unfortunately he does a pretty good job of convincing us. Too many precious sons and daughters of God are bound by these unbiblical thoughts and attitudes about themselves. So often, we don't recognize the seeds of doubt about our identity and God's character. Part of the reason we are easily swayed by such thinking is that we don't know the truth of God's Word. We have not brought our minds under the instruction of His Word. Dear friend, please do not believe these lies. If you give them an ounce of credit they essentially put you in mental wheelchairs, holding you back from becoming the person God wants you to be. Instead, make every effort to learn and believe what the Bible says about what God really thinks about you:

> I pray that you, being rooted and established in love, may have power, together with all the saints, to grasp how wide and long and high and deep is the love of Christ, and to know this love that surpasses knowledge—that you may be filled to the measure of all the fullness of God (Ephesians 3:17–19).

God wants you to know how much He loves and values you, how all your sins are taken away, and how He desires to use your life for His great purposes. Don't let negative thinking hold you back from entering into God's wonderful plan for your life.

Beloved, how you think about yourself is important, for God does not want you to be bound by such unhealthy attitudes and strongholds of the mind. You are precious to God and nothing on this earth, other than the lies you wrongly believe about yourself, will stop Him from using your life for a great purpose.

Wrong Thoughts about God

If the devil can't get you by making you feel awful about yourself, then he'll try another method: to sabotage how you think and feel about God. In other words, he will try to turn your heart away from God through doubting and disbelieving His goodness, faithfulness, and love.

Why is it we are so ready to believe God orchestrates all the evil in the world and we never hear the devil, the real author of evil, blamed for it? We too easily believe lies such as these about God and His character:

- God is indifferent to the needs of people.
- He is too hard to please.
- The Bible is not realistic for living in today's world.
- God is not at work in suffering.
- God is far off.
- God doesn't really care about you.

- God's promises are not real for today.
- God will not answer your prayers.
- God doesn't heal today.
- God caused your friend to become sick.

There is no truth to any of these statements, yet many of us believe at least one or two of them. That's all it takes to immobilize us in our relationships with God. The devil knows full well that if we believe what God's Word says and believe in the goodness of God, he's in trouble. A Christian who believes the truth about God can shake this world for Him, and the devil doesn't want that to happen.

1. What are some ideas you have about God and His will for you that you suspect may not be true and Biblical?

_____

_____

An anemic view of yourself or of God will prevent you from growing and maturing in Him, and fulfilling His purposes in your life. So how can such unhealthy and wrong thinking change? The good news is, with God's help, it can.

Renew Your Thinking

As Sungjoo shared in the opening testimony, God wants to bring healing and hope into our lives. To accomplish that, He wants to change, purify, and, where necessary, rectify wrong thought patterns we have become accustomed to. This happens as we put off our old selves and are made new in the attitudes of our minds. In other words, *we need to reeducate our thought life through the Word of God.*

I don't know if you realize this, but you have power over and the ability to change how you think. It may not seem like that sometimes, but according to these verses of Ephesians 4, it is possible to become new in the thinking and attitudes of our mind. If that weren't the case, then surely those verses wouldn't be there.

How exactly does that happen? How are our minds renewed? It's not simply a matter of pushing away wrong thoughts. That would merely tire us out. Instead, we need to proactively put new thoughts into our minds to replace the old. The next time you find yourself thinking something you know isn't right, don't just struggle to push that thought aside. Replace it with a good and true thought from Scripture. By way of personal example, whenever I find myself tempted to go down the path of negative thinking about myself, I ask God to bring to mind a Bible verse that speaks the truth. Instead of focusing on the wrong perception or attitude, I mull over and meditate on what God says. By doing that, I renew my thinking, and as with any habit, it will eventually become more natural.

The next time you discern a lie about who you are or about the love and goodness of God, find an appropriate Scripture and meditate on that instead. Go one step further and declare it aloud. It's surprisingly powerful and effective.

Don't readily believe the lies of the enemy, an enemy who is trying to discourage you and hold you back from running with God. Instead, immerse your thinking in the truth of God's Word, which has the power to change wrong and negative thought patterns. Help your attitudes become renewed by allowing God's Word to fill your heart and mind, which will revolutionize negative thinking about yourself, others, God, and His plans for you. As you allow God's Word to change and renew your thinking, you are made new, the old man or woman disappears, and a new creation in Christ is born. If you are willing to renew your thinking, you can positively change and renew your whole life.[2]

2. What is one area of negative thinking you sometimes struggle with?

_____

_____

3. Find one Scripture that speaks the truth about that belief and meditate on it for the next twenty-four hours.

_____

_____

MAKE OR BREAK

For where your treasure is, there your heart will be also.
—Matthew 6:21

As we have seen, one of the most influential aspects of our character that determines success or failure in any discipline and area of life is our attitude. To a very large extent, our attitudes are an expression of who we are, what we really believe, and what we are living for. For this reason, our attitudes will also greatly affect the quality of our relationship with God.

Attitude Determines Destiny

> *For as he thinks in his heart, so is he.*
> —Proverbs 23:7, NKJV

As these verses of Matthew and Proverbs reveal, how we think and what we value become who we essentially are. It therefore follows that we need to pay careful attention to the attitudes of our heart and mind.

One example of the effect of unhealthy attitudes and values is seen in the early church, where the apostle Paul encountered problems of spiritual immaturity among believers. They had started off so well in their faith, following Jesus Christ wholeheartedly, and had been enjoying the blessings of community with fellow believers. On the outside things seemed to be going well. However, a closer look revealed things were beginning to unravel. Their ongoing progress was being hampered and things were not what they should have been:

> Brothers, I could not address you as spiritual but as worldly—mere infants in Christ. I gave you milk, not solid food, for you were not ready for it. Indeed,

you are still not ready. You are still worldly. For since there is jealously and quarreling among you, are you not worldly? Are you not acting like mere men? For when one says, "I follow Paul," and another, "I follow Apollos," are you not mere men? (1 Corinthians 3:1–4).

How embarrassing. Imagine being rebuked for your immaturity and worldliness as a disciple of Christ. For some reason, these believers had taken a reversal in their spiritual growth and were now failing to mature in their relationship with God. Paul likened their lifestyle and behavior to that of unbelievers, seen in their immature attitudes toward one another. They were no longer focused on following Christ but had set their attentions on the things of the world instead. Their attitudes and actions were completely off, their spiritual maturity stunted.

Our attitude has everything to do with how we progress in our faith. It will make you or break you. You alone are responsible for nurturing your spiritual growth. In the following parable, Jesus talked about individual responsibility for spiritual development:

A farmer went out to sow his seed. As he was scattering the seed, some fell along the path; it was trampled on, and the birds of the air ate it up. Some fell on rock, and when it came up, the plants withered because they had no moisture. Other seed fell among thorns, which grew up with it and choked the plants. Still other seed fell on good soil. It came up and yielded a crop, a hundred times more than was sown. ...

This is the meaning of the parable: The seed is the word of God. Those along the path are the ones who hear, and then the devil comes and takes away the word from their hearts, so that they may not believe and be saved. Those on the rock are the ones who receive the word with joy when they hear it, but they have no root. They believe for a while, but in the time of testing they fall away. The seed that fell among thorns stands for those who hear, but as they go on their way they are choked by life's worries, riches and pleasures, and they do not mature. But the seed on good soil stands for those with a noble and good heart, who hear the word, retain it, and by persevering produce a crop (Luke 8:5–8, 11–15).

This parable teaches that how you respond to God's Word in your life is *your* responsibility and will determine your level of maturity. Nobody else can make you grow; only you can foster that. Although each person in this story received the Word of God equally, in the end it was how each person chose to respond to God's Word that made all the difference in what kind of crop they produced. It was their attitude and subsequent conduct in the face of tests and trials that determined whether they grew and bore fruit or not. Ben discussed the importance of maintaining a right attitude:

> The key thing I've learned from being a leader and chaplain in basketball is the importance of having good composure, good peace. Just as in life where things can go up and down, the game too can swing so easily from the momentum in your team or the other team. I have found that your ability to keep composure in those times will keep a steady incline while you're going through things. Not just flat composure, but a positive one.

In our walk with God, hanging on to a positive and hopeful attitude in difficult seasons will enable us to draw near to God and find our strength in Him. Friend, what kind of person are you? Are you the kind who hears God's Word and yet, because of hardness, it cannot penetrate or take root in your life? Whenever you hear God's Word, does Satan quickly snatch it away so no roots can develop?

Or are you like the second category of people in Jesus' parable? Although your faith experience started with much joy and excitement, are you now beginning to fall under a time of testing because you have no roots? Despite your initial enthusiasm about Jesus, have you failed to grow spiritually and, as a result, whatever life you once had is quickly evaporating?

Perhaps you're more like the third category of people Jesus described who allowed the thorns of this world to choke out their faith. You believe the difficulties and temptations are too strong and are drawing you away from God. Friend, if you will make the choice to depend on the promises of God's Word, you will not only develop the roots you need to stand and grow spiritually, but you will experience the power of God in your life. If you don't, your faith is in real danger of having the life completely choked out of it.

Whichever category we find ourselves in, deep down we all desire to become like the fourth category of people Jesus described. The good news is it's never too late. It is entirely possible to not allow the cares or pleasures of this world to destroy our faith, but learn how to draw near to God and experience Him and His power through such times. As you choose to respond with an attitude of faith and trust in the face of life's thorns, I promise you will grow in your faith and relationship with God. I'm not merely talking about having an increase of nice, fuzzy feelings of faith and peace. I'm talking about experiencing God working in your life and answering your prayers. In other words, you can witness the miracles of God, big and small, in your life. When you begin to experience God in these ways, you will be able to withstand the storms and tests that come your way.

Your attitude toward God's Word and your response to Him will determine the direction of your spiritual experience. So where is your greatest treasure? What do you care about most? Are weeds choking your faith and overwhelming you? It doesn't have to be that way. Remember, it's how you respond to God's Word, whether you choose to obey, that determines whether or not you grow spiritually and survive the storms of life. If you are willing to put God first, making Him your first love, He will take care of you. Nothing is greater than knowing God in a real and tangible way. Nothing compares to running with God. Anything else is just an empty counterfeit.

4. What do you think God desires you to do with the concerns and needs of your daily life?

_____

_____

5. In your opinion, why is it important to have an attitude of complete trust in God and His Word?

_____

_____

6. Why do you think it's important to guard our attitudes toward the things of God and His Word?

_____

_____

GREATER EXPECTATIONS

I tell you the truth, anyone who has faith in me will do what I have been doing. He will do even greater things than these, because I am going to the Father. And I will do whatever you ask in my name, so that the Son may bring glory to the Father. You may ask me for anything in my name, and I will do it.
—John 14:12–14

Jesus spoke often about God's desire that we place our faith in Him. To live the Christian life as a fit and strong athlete of God, it is essential you learn how to live by faith, trusting God's Word. An attitude of faith is fundamental to your relationship with God and your experience of Him moving in your life.

According to the words of Jesus Christ, the person who lives by faith will see God do great works. These include seeing prayers answered, sins forgiven, lives restored, the sick healed, mountains moved, the gospel preached, practical needs met, and, as a result, the wonderful glory of God witnessed. As we live by faith and see the awesome deeds of God, God is greatly glorified and people are drawn closer to Him. However, a heart of doubt and unbelief will have the exact opposite effect.

As Christians we are supposed to hold one particular value, which stands us apart from those who don't follow God: we believe in the power and love of God. However—and let's be honest about this—there are too many unbelieving believers in the church today. Ask yourself, do you believe what Jesus said in the opening verses of John 14? Do you believe that if you have faith in God you will be able to continue the works of Jesus Christ in this world? Probably many of us would not be able to give a wholehearted yes to those questions.

Yet what else could Jesus have intended when He spoke these words? Surely He simply meant what He said, that *if* we believe, we will also do what He did. Have you ever noticed how often Jesus validated many of His profound statements with the words, "I tell you the truth"? Why would Jesus make such bold promises if they weren't true? Dear friend, we need to stop questioning the promises of God and live like we believe so God our Father will be glorified.

When we do not live like we believe what God's Word says, the result is a powerless life that doesn't bring God anywhere near as much honor and glory than if we did believe His Word. Too many of us are willing to settle for a mediocre Christian experience, unaware of the fact that God wants to do mighty miracles *today* in order to usher in His kingdom here on earth and glorify Himself. God wants to use *you* to do His mighty works here on this earth, things that are beyond your imagination.

I believe the church of the West today has much to learn from the church of the East. In the Middle East, China, and Africa, among other places in the world, many are coming to faith in Jesus Christ through experiencing a miracle either in their own lives or the lives of sick loved ones. In the Middle East, around one-third of Muslim converts come to faith after having experienced Jesus Christ appearing to them in a dream or vision. We in the West may have great resources and structures in our churches, but the believers in Asian and African countries are leaps ahead of us when it comes to living by faith and subsequently experiencing the power and miracles of God. Friend, we need to harness the best of both churches.

In his book, *Dreams and Visions: Is Jesus Awakening the Muslim World?* Tom Doyle shares countless testimonies of people coming to faith after having an encounter with God:

> "You're the one!" A woman's shout broke above the pandemonium of Cairo's Khan el-Khalili Friday Market.

"You're the one!"

Kamal Assam spun toward the voice. His eyes fixed on the black hijab walking toward him. A female hand protruded from the full-body covering, pointing in his direction.

"You were in my dream last night." The woman, now close enough to be heard without shouting, breathed heavily from the effort of pushing through the mob and from her own shock at the unfolding mystery of her circumstances.

"Those clothes. You were wearing those clothes. For sure, it was you."

"Was I with Jesus?" he asked.

"Yes," the woman cried, "Jesus was with us!"

What had begun as an atypical visit for him to the Friday Market had just taken an even more uncanny and exciting turn. That morning while reading his Bible, Kamal felt a compelling urge to leave his house where he was staying and venture to the Friday Market.

"Jesus walked with me alongside a lake, and He told me how much He loves me." The woman in black told Kamal details of the vivid dream she'd had the night before their meeting.[3]

For the next three hours, Kamal shared the gospel of Jesus Christ with this Muslim mother of eight. Yet this story is not uncommon. Jesus, it seems, it taking the initiative of introducing Himself in places where the gospel is not easily heard, leading many to embark on a journey of seeking the Way, the Truth, and the Life.

Have Greater Expectations

We need to have greater expectations of God. A person who refuses to take God at His Word and live by faith will have few encounters with God, which in turn brings little glory to God. A lack of faith in God's love today inhibits God's power from manifesting among us, an experience that even Jesus encountered in His hometown:

> Jesus said to them, "Only in his hometown, among his relatives and in his own house is a prophet without honor." He could not do any miracles there, except lay his hands on a few sick people and heal them. And he was amazed at their lack of faith (Mark 6:4–6).

The townsfolk were familiar with Jesus. They had grown up with Him and, because of their familiarity, refused to believe He had a divine anointing. As a result of their lack of faith and expectations, Jesus was not able to do many miracles. That's the fruit of an unbelieving attitude.

However, God's power *is* released when we operate in the realm of faith, as many are seeing around the world today. When you are willing to exercise the faith you have, no matter how small, God responds. When God moves in power in our lives, then our loved ones, whether Christians or not, are drawn closer to God, and our great God is glorified. Don't we all want that? I know I do. As John Dawson aptly states:

Who is your God? Is He the God of the Bible? Your
God is only as big as what you expect of Him in
space and time. What do you expect Him to do here
on earth in this generation? Don't tell me about the
God of your theology. It's easy to say that He's all-
powerful, but do you expect Him to do powerful
things here and now?[4]

God's power is released when we operate in faith.

Let's decide today to stop believing God for so little and
let's increase our expectations of Him. Perhaps you've yet
to see a miracle, or perhaps you have even been taught that
such things don't happen today. Whatever your experience,
I want to encourage you to start believing what the Bible
promises and start running with God. Be willing to put
yourself out there and take risks, following God's leading and
promptings as Kamal did. Consider Simon Peter: "'Lord, if
it's you,' Peter replied, 'tell me to come to you on the water.'
'Come,' he said. Then Peter got down out of the boat, walked
on the water and came toward Jesus" (Matthew 14:28–29).

Simon Peter was the only disciple who was willing to
get out of the boat and experience the impossible. All the
other disciples were too afraid to step out of their comfort
zone. What kind of disciple do you want to be? Are you
willing to get out of your boat and be stretched?

I don't know about you, but I don't want to live a pseudo-
Christian life. I haven't come this far and made the sacrifices
I've made for that kind of Christian experience. Brothers and
sisters, it's time to expand our thinking of what God can

do among us today. It's time to have an attitude of faith and start believing the Word of God and living like we believe it. It's time to become believing believers like Charles and Frances Hunter.

Charles and Frances were a wonderful couple who preached the gospel to millions and saw countless healings by the power of the Holy Spirit right to the end of their lives. Toward the end of her life, reflecting on her remarkable journey with God, Frances shared these words:

> The Christian life is the most exciting life in the world. There are only two things you need to do. Number one, do what God tells you to do. Number two, don't do what He tells you not to do. Now, that is the whole secret. It's that simple.
>
> To me, living the Christian life is not a bunch of ups and downs. I think that it takes a total sell-out to Jesus so that nothing else makes a difference. Charles and I do not *talk* about anything else; we do not *do* anything else; and since I was saved, I never *had* anything else.[5]

They understood from God's Word that when Jesus walked here on this earth, He preached the whole kingdom of God. He showed its power to save, heal, and deliver, and they believed through their study of the Scriptures that God's will is no different today. People's needs are no different today. I could list at least thirty people I know and care for who need God and His touch upon their lives. I'm sure you could, too.

7. Read Ephesians 1:18–20. What do these verses teach about how our hearts need to be enlightened?

_____

_____

8. Why do you think we need this?

_____

_____

The writer of Ephesians explained how these believers needed enlightenment and clarification on what they were called to and what spiritual resources they had. We need the same explanations today. God wants you to know that you too have God's riches and great power at your disposal because you are a child of the King.

God desires to seek and save the lost today, and the Bible teaches that if we will believe and ask Him for what we need, He will give us what we ask. As we do, God our Father will be glorified just as He was when Jesus walked the earth, performing all those miracles. I want to encourage you to pray and ask God to expand your thinking on what He desires to do in and through your life. Ask God to open the eyes of _your_ heart to the power of His Word. There is a lost world out there and you and I are commissioned to preach the gospel of Jesus Christ in all its fullness. Are you willing to run with the baton for your generation? Will you

give your best to your race? You will be surprised at what
God can do through you:

> Now to him who is able to do immeasurably more
> than all we ask or imagine, according to his power
> that is at work within us, to him be the glory in the
> church and in Christ Jesus throughout all genera-
> tions, for ever and ever! (Ephesians 3:20–21).

9. What do you think a life of faith should look like?

_____

_____

CONFIDENT IN GOD

*But Moses said to God, "Who am I that I should go
to Pharaoh and bring the Israelites out of Egypt?"*
—Exodus 3:11

One common hindrance that prevents believers from
fully walking into God's purposes for their lives derives
from a lack of confidence in their ability to succeed in
fulfilling God's purposes. They feel God is calling them
to do something, but they are afraid and hesitant to do it.
They're not alone.

In the Bible we find numerous examples of individuals
who lacked confidence, one being Moses, as the opening verse in this section shows. As mentioned earlier, if

God had called Moses to this great deliverance mission decades earlier, He would have encountered a confident, well-educated young man who was "powerful in speech and action" (Acts 7:22).

But something changed during Moses' years of exile in the desert and his fall from Egyptian prince to humble shepherd that prepared him for God's work. In a strange turn of events, his humbling experiences brought him to a place where he was exhausted of his own ambition and strength. He no longer felt confident and bold. So when God called Moses to bring His people out of slavery, he was reluctant and didn't believe he had what it took to fulfill this divine calling. He is not the only one.

Gideon also struggled to believe God could use him for a great task. When the angel of the living God commissioned him to deliver the Israelites from the hands of their enemies, the Midianites, Gideon grumbled. The conversation is enlightening:

> When the angel of the Lord appeared to Gideon, he said, "the Lord is with you, mighty warrior."
>
> "But sir," Gideon replied, "if the Lord is with us, why has all this happened to us? Where are all his wonders that our fathers told us about when they said, 'Did not the Lord bring us up out of Egypt?' But now the Lord has abandoned us and put us into the hand of Midian."
>
> The Lord turned to him and said, "Go in the strength you have and save Israel out of Midian's hand. Am I not sending you?"

"But Lord," Gideon asked, "how can I save Israel? My clan is the weakest in Manasseh, and I am the least in my family."

The Lord answered, "I will be with you, and you will strike down all the Midianites together" (Judges 6:12–16).

From these verses we see God didn't choose Gideon because of his great strength and talents. God saw potential in him, just as he saw in Moses, despite his weaknesses.

Correct Perception

How God viewed Gideon and how Gideon viewed himself were polar opposites. God addressed Gideon as "mighty warrior," but Gideon saw himself as anything but that. In fact, Gideon described himself as the least man among the weakest clan. You can't get a lower opinion of yourself than that.

Do you relate to Gideon? Perhaps you see yourself contrary to how God views you, and you lack confidence in what God is calling you to do. Dear friend, the devil prowls around like a roaring lion seeking to destroy the work of God in us (1 Peter 5:8), and some of his most effective weapons include insecurity and doubt about who we are and what God wants to do in our lives. I love the story of my friend Joohee and how God answered her prayer for guidance for her future:

God is faithful and He speaks to people who trust Him! I experienced this by going through the process of deciding which graduate school to attend. Although I had received offers from all the schools I had applied to, I really wanted to know what God's will was, but I was having difficulty in hearing from Him and discerning His will for me.

At that time, I was taking a course at church on how to find God's purpose for your life. During one of the sessions we were taught that when making big decisions in life we need to receive confirmation from God in three areas: Scripture, the Holy Spirit, and our practical circumstances. I really wanted to get confirmation from God about choosing a school, so I started to earnestly pray about it. For almost a month, I could not hear anything special from God. There was no Bible verse that stood out to me or prompting that seemed to be from the Holy Spirit. The deadline to decide which offer was fast approaching and I felt frustrated as I saw time was running out. But I did not want to give up hope on receiving confirmation from God.

One evening I talked to the course pastor about the frustration I felt, and I asked her to pray for me. She reminded me of God's goodness and faithfulness, and she encouraged me to continue to trust that God would answer me. After I received her prayer, I felt peace inside and I suddenly had a strong feeling God would speak to me in time.

On my way back home, the peace in my heart grew more and more and I felt excitement surging up in my heart. As I was enjoying these feelings, I received a message from my dad. He told me to call him because he had something to say about one of the schools.

I was not sure what to expect because my dad had been strongly opposed to me going abroad to study. We even had a huge argument a few months earlier and he was negative about the idea of studying in Europe and the subject I was hoping to study. Eventually he had reluctantly approved of my study plans.

So I called my dad without much expectation. To my surprise, he said he had spent more than an hour reading online about the program in Italy and concluded that it was perfect for me. Over the phone, his voice sounded full of excitement and certainty. Even more, he strongly recommended that I choose this program over all the others. I was blown away!

Even though I was joyful to experience this, I wanted to make sure I received confirmation from all three sources, including Scripture. I still had the strong belief God would answer me in time, so I continued to wait prayerfully. That week I was reviewing and meditating on some verses quoted in Sunday sermons and my pastor's course. As I was reading them over and over again, Joshua 1:9 stood out to me:

> Have I not commanded you? Be strong and courageous. Do not be frightened, and do not be dismayed, for the Lord your God is with you wherever you go.

Gradually God started to speak words of courage into my heart. I felt God was telling me to be courageous and not fearful of anything because He was going to be with me. Comparing the Italian program to other ones, everything seemed tougher. The curriculum, graduation requirements, visa issuance, housing arrangement, and many other aspects were more complicated and challenging. Even though I liked the Italian program, I was afraid of potential obstacles I could foresee. However, the more I meditated on the verse, the more I felt strengthened to face these challenges. Eventually, I realized God wanted me to grow and experience Him on a whole new level through the more challenging program in Italy.

The next day I contacted the school in Italy and accepted their offer. Until this moment I still had God's peace in my heart. It's difficult to describe, but I felt a combination of peace, love, and joy that filled my heart so full that it was impossible to find even a hole in it.

I'm glad I continued to trust God and wait on Him to speak to me. If I had given in to doubt, I would have missed the opportunity to receive God's confirmation in making an important decision in my life. Instead I felt the joy of experiencing God's guidance and I grew much closer to Him through the process. Now I'm looking forward to experiencing God more and becoming more intimate with Him. I'm excited for the things God will show me in Italy and beyond.

Although Joohee initially experienced doubt about whether God would speak to her and reveal His will for her life, she persevered and chose to place her faith and trust in Him. God wants to do the same for you: to give you confidence in Him and in His relationship with you.

Take a minute to read the following statements and ask yourself how many you really accept:

- I am loved and accepted by God.
- God has a wonderful plan for my life.
- God has forgiven every single one of my past sins.
- I am in right standing before God.
- I am God's son or daughter.
- God wants to speak to me and reveal His will to me.
- I have God's Holy Spirit and power within me.
- I have enough faith to move mountains.
- Nothing can separate me from God's love.
- God listens to and answers my prayers.

I expect all of us have doubted these Biblical truths at one time or another. We have little problem believing them for others, but for ourselves, that's a different story. Yet is there any reason why God should treat you differently than any other of His children? The fact is, God will keep every single one of His promises *to you* as you walk in obedience to His ways. There's no reason to doubt that. It's time to replace some of that wrong thinking with the truth of God's Word.

Read through the following chart to recognize the lies of our enemy and believe the truths of God's Word.

Lie	Truth of Scripture
I am not loved by God.	How great is the love the Father has lavished on us, that we should be called children of God! (1 John 3:1).
God has no purpose for my life.	For we are God's workmanship, created in Christ Jesus to do good works, which God prepared in advance for us to do (Ephesians 2:10).
I cannot receive clear guidance from God.	Trust in the Lord with all your heart; do not depend on your own understanding. Seek his will in all you do, and he will show you which path to take (Proverbs 3:5–6 NLT).
I have little strength.	I can do everything through him who gives me strength (Philippians 4:13).
I don't have enough money.	But seek first his kingdom and his righteousness and all these things will be given to you as well (Matthew 6:33).
God doesn't really care about me.	Cast all your anxiety on him because he cares for you (1 Peter 5:7).
I feel sinful.	He saved us through the washing of rebirth and renewal by the Holy Spirit (Titus 3:5).
God still counts my sins against me.	He will not always accuse. … As far as the east is from the west, so far has he removed our transgressions from us (Psalm 103:9,12).

Correct Dependence

Whenever we estimate our ability to do what God has called us to do based on our own abilities, then it's no wonder we are hesitant or lack confidence. Whatever God calls you to do, He will equip you to do. He's not looking for perfect vessels, but people who are willing to place their confidence in Him, not in themselves alone.

When we tell God we are not able or willing to do what He is calling us to do, that shows we are putting our confidence in the wrong place: we don't feel strong enough, therefore we conclude we will fail, and so we'd better not try at all. Beloved, the Bible clearly shows that when God calls someone to a great task, He doesn't expect that person to fulfill it in his or her own strength. Where would the glory for God be in that? Whatever God calls you to do, He promises to empower you for. All God is looking from you is an attitude of willingness to obey and step out. He will do the rest.

I know that whenever God asks me to do something, I am inadequate for the task, so I don't waste time meditating on my inabilities or weaknesses. Nor do I allow how I feel to excuse me from obedience. Instead, when I absolutely know I cannot do what God is calling me to do, I let go of the reins and say, "OK God. I can't do this. I need your help."

When we have this attitude of utter reliance and dependence on God, that's precisely when we see and experience God's power. Many days in church ministry were so full of meetings and pastoral commitments that I found myself saying to God, "I really haven't got what it takes for today, Lord. Over to you." I never despaired at such moments. In fact, it was actually very releasing and brought great peace because I stopped worrying, and I trusted God to make up for what I was lacking. I simply didn't allow myself to become anxious about my inadequacies. I believed God was with me and that was all I needed. I *knew* He would help me, and He always did. I actually went through those kind of days with much less stress because my dependence was totally on God and not on myself.

When God asks you to do something, He doesn't expect you to fight the battle by yourself. As God told Gideon, He will be with you and He will help you. I love how God reassured His people in 2 Chronicles 20:15: "Do not be afraid or discouraged because of this vast army. For the battle is not yours, but God's."

Understand that your felt weakness actually gives God the opportunity to work through you, not by might nor by power, but by God's Spirit (Zechariah 4:6). There were times when even the great apostle Paul felt weak, but he saw such times as opportunities for God's power to be experienced and displayed: "But he said to me, 'My grace is sufficient for you, for my power is made perfect in weakness.' Therefore I will boast all the more gladly about my weaknesses, so that Christ's power may rest on me" (2 Corinthians 12:9).

Paul didn't allow his feelings of weakness or inadequacy stop him from serving God. Instead, he actually reveled and boasted in his weaknesses.

When Gideon and Moses informed God of how weak or inadequate they felt, it didn't change God's mind about choosing them. He didn't turn around and say, "Oh, you're right. You're too weak to do this task after all. I'd better find someone stronger and more suitable." Instead, He wanted them, just as He wants us, to experience His power and grow in confidence in Him.

Stop putting the focus on your abilities and strength. It doesn't matter whether you lack confidence; what matters is whether you are trusting God to enable you. We can all hide behind our weaknesses, but that is not the Biblical way. Yes, you may very well be too weak, but that doesn't matter to God, for it serves as a golden opportunity for God to show His power. All God wants from you is a willing and obedient attitude. Put your confidence not in yourself, but in God, just as David did when faced with fearful situations: "The Lord who delivered me from the paw of the lion and the paw of the bear will deliver me from the hand of the Philistine" (1 Samuel 17:37).

If you are willing to take the first step, you will immediately see God move, because God responds to your attitude of faith. Your weakness is the perfect channel for God's strength.

10. What was the difference between David's confidence and that of Moses and Gideon in what we read?

_____

_____

11. What reason have you been using as to why God cannot use you for His purposes? What does the Bible say about that?

_____

_____

12. Where is your confidence placed?

_____

_____

OBEDIENCE AND HUMILITY

Then Jesus said to his disciples, "If anyone would come after me, he must deny himself and take up his cross and follow me. For whoever wants to save his life will lose it, but whoever loses his life for me will find it. ... For the Son of Man is going to come in his Father's glory with his angels, and then he will reward each person according to what he has done."
—Matthew 16:24–27

The fact you are reading this book reveals the wonderful truth that you desire to grow in God and the knowledge of His love and power for you. Dear reader, let me share the following important truth with you: you learn more through obedience than by mere knowledge alone.

We learn more through obedience than knowledge.

However, obedience doesn't always come easy, and it requires discipline and even, at times, sacrifice. Jesus wasn't joking when he told us to take up our crosses to follow Him. Obedience to God will sometimes require us to die to our own selfish wants.

No Pain, No Gain

All athletes know that embarking on a course of intense training and discipline is going to require some sacrifice, sweat, and exertion. No true sportsperson would ever expect to improve and succeed in accomplishing his or her goals without it. Wins don't come easily but are the result of intense training and discipline. "No pain, no gain," as the saying goes.

This principle of growth is especially true in the area of building muscle. To build and strengthen muscle, the muscle fibers have to first be broken down, which happens through strenuous exercise, pushing yourself until you feel the strain and discomfort. When you feel your muscles hurting, you know the exercise is doing its work and the fibers are being torn down. Later as they repair and heal, the muscles become stronger than before. As author and personal trainer Mark Vella writes,

> In order to gain improvement in fitness, the body must be stimulated beyond its current capacity. Therefore, if you wish to gain strength, you must train with a weight stimulus that is higher than your current capacity. This amount of stimulus is called the overload. Too great an overload can, however, cause injury.[6]

This is a great analogy to learn from. Doesn't it feel sometimes as if God is allowing us to go through pressure and painful circumstances beyond our current ability? We cannot get away from the fact that the Bible does talk about being disciplined by God, yet his discipline is not malicious or unkind. Quite the opposite: God disciplines us because He loves us and wants to change us for the better:

> "My son, do not make light of the Lord's discipline, and do not lose heart when he rebukes you, because the Lord disciplines those he loves, and he punishes everyone he accepts as a son."
>
> Endure hardship as discipline; God is treating you as sons. For what son is not disciplined by his father? ... Our fathers disciplined us for a little while as they thought best; but God disciplines us for our good, that we may share in his holiness. No discipline seems pleasant at the time, but painful. Later on, however, it produces a harvest of righteousness and peace for those who have been trained by it (Hebrews 12:5–11).

The Wineskin Principle

God desires that we share in His holiness, and that can only happen through change. Matthew 9:17 had me stumped for many years. In that verse, Jesus talked about the dangers of pouring new wine into old wineskins, and how new wine should only be poured into new wineskins if both are to be preserved. Jesus was explaining how God was doing things in a new way under the New Covenant, that knowing God was not a matter of mere external rituals and law-keeping. Under this New Covenant of Jesus Christ, to know God and experience His new life, the inner man must be changed.

As we make room, God brings newness of life.

Friend, what I've since learned is that God can only pour His new life into new vessels. That's what He meant about pouring new wine (life through His Spirit) into new wineskins (our lives). I call it the "wineskin principle": God brings newness of life in us as we make room for Him by being willing to get rid of the old, for our old man cannot contain the new. That's why we need to be willing to repent of our sins and allow God to form our new character. Don't misunderstand me: I'm not saying you have to change your life first and then God can work. I'm simply saying you have to be willing to repent; God will do the rest. Change begins with a decision.

God's Classroom

As many of us know too well, God will often allow us to undergo tough seasons to forge and bring about His loving discipline and education into our lives. Think about it: someone prays and asks God to make them more patient. Does God just download this characteristic into us like something from *The Matrix* movie? Of course not, though that would be nicer! Instead, He uses challenging circumstances to give us the opportunity to *learn* patience. Whether it's increased faith, love, trust, patience, kindness, or whatever the quality may be, we grow through moments of discipline—*if* we are willing to go with the plan, as my friend Alison found:

> For a few years post-university, I was living and working overseas. There I became connected with

a thriving church, which God used to turn my life around and draw me back to Himself. Those few years saw the formation of some deep Christian friendships and a passion to live my life the way God intended me to. After three years, however, I felt God call me back home to Canada. As excited as I was to be reacquainted with my family, I was incredibly sad to leave my friends and nervous about returning home with no clear indication of what was next.

After the initial excitement of being home wore off, reality set in and I found myself in a very dark place. I had virtually no community in my small town. I wasn't sure what kind of vocation to pursue, and job hunting was a long and painful process. As well, after being highly independent for the last few years, it was a real struggle to move back with my parents. I felt like I was seriously regressing in life, as if I had been dropped into a giant void. I wasn't prepared for the intensity of it.

If I didn't have my faith through that season, I may have lost all hope. But I was determined to push through it and trust God, and God was faithful in encouraging me. In some of my darkest moments, God shone a light on some key verses that would carry me through. When I read Hosea 2:14–16, God acknowledged the desert season I was in but spoke of a time when things would be restored. God used Habakkuk 2:2–3 to urge me to hold on, wait for the good things that were to come, and trust in His promise. Jeremiah 29:10–13 and 1 Peter 5:10 reminded me to put my hope in God and His goodness.

In total, my unemployment lasted seven months. When a job finally did materialize, I was incredibly thankful and could see that it was indeed worth waiting for. God answered my prayers for direction through that and enabled me to start building skills for my career.

Unfortunately, ten months later the door closed unexpectedly on that job, and I realized I would have to start job hunting again. With that dark season still fresh in my memory, I wasn't thrilled to be back in that same place. However, this time I was much less fearful about what was to come. God had taught me the previous year that He is always in control and things will always work out for our good if we put our trust in Him. I was able to look back and remember how faithful God had been in providing for me, and I completely trusted that things were going to work out just fine. And they did.

As hard as it was to persevere through that season, I'm so thankful God loved me enough to have me go through it. Through that experience I now have a much deeper trust in God and am better equipped to deal with things in a healthy way.

Although it was difficult for Alison to go through that dark time, she experienced the comfort and faithfulness of God and is now a stronger woman of God because of it. She came through it successfully because she chose to draw near to God and trust Him despite how hopeless things seemed.

God uses challenging circumstances in our lives to teach and mature us, purify and strengthen us. When we are faced with such situations, the challenge always is, will we trust and obey? If we are willing, we will see the fruit and harvest of our obedience. But if we are not willing and give up partway, we can only expect to have to resit the exam at some point later on. And who wants to do that? Even Jesus had to learn this valuable lesson of obedience: "Although he was a son, he learned obedience from what he suffered and, once made perfect, he became the source of eternal salvation" (Hebrews 5:8–9).

The Relationship between Humility and Obedience

Another important aspect in this area of obedience is that it is only possible for the person who is willing to walk the path of humility. I'm not talking about a lowly, unhealthy opinion of ourselves, but rather the attitude of acknowledging our utter dependence on God and the laying down of our own desires for the benefit of another.

Obedience is only possible through humility.

You see, in God's kingdom, we will not be judged by how many people served us but by how many people we served. A humble person seeks to please and obey God just as Jesus did:

Your attitude should be the same as that of Christ Jesus: Who, being in very nature God, did not consider equality with God something to be grasped, but made himself nothing, taking the very nature of a servant, being made in human likeness. And being found in appearance as a man, he humbled himself and became obedient to death—even death on a cross! (Philippians 2:5–8).

Because He was willing to be humbled, He was able to obey the Father. Obedience and humility are interrelated; we cannot obey God without humility. Not only that, but obedience also proves our love for God: "This is how we know that we love the children of God: by loving God and carrying out his commands. This is love for God: to obey his commands. And his commands are not burdensome, for everyone born of God overcomes the world" (1 John 5:2–4).

The Bible teaches that only those who have an attitude of obedience toward God are those who truly love Him. In other words, our obedience and humility are marks of true discipleship: "Why do you call me, 'Lord, Lord,' and do not do what I say?" (Luke 6:46).

Calling Jesus Christ our Lord while not taking obedience to Him seriously reveals that we are only living for ourselves and not for the will and purpose of God. As John Bevere warns,

> The reference to *Lord* in the above verse originates from the Greek word *kurios*. Strong's dictionary of Greek words defines it as "supreme in authority or master." Jesus meant that there would be those who confess Him as Lord but do not follow Him as their supreme authority.

They live in a manner that does not support what they confess. They obey the will of God as long as it does not conflict with the desires of their own heart. If the will of God takes them in a different direction than the one they desire, they choose their own path yet still call Jesus "Lord."[7]

As Jesus taught in Matthew 16, to truly follow Him will require our willingness to deny ourselves and take up our crosses daily. That is not a bad thing, for as we lay down our own desires and ambitions in trusting God, He gives us His own in their place, which are always much better than we could ever create.

One of the biggest sacrifices I've had to make was when God called me to leave my home and family back in beautiful Wales and move to the other side of the world without even knowing why. When I first told my family (who were not believers), they couldn't understand my decision to move to Far East Asia. Why would I want to give up my job and leave my lovely house, car, and cat to go to the other side of the globe where I couldn't even speak the language? It seemed so illogical to everyone, reinforced by the fact that my parents were getting older and it seemed like I was abandoning them. It was a hard decision, but when it came down to it, I realized I just had to lay down my own will and concerns and simply trust God to take care of the rest.

It's been eleven years since the move and now it makes perfect sense. In South Korea God gave me a wonderful career in church ministry and an amazing husband. Moreover, God has taken wonderful care of my parents, far better than I ever could have.

God rewards obedience, my friend, and He desires to give you the best, but this can only happen if you have an attitude of humility and trust. As you follow God wherever He leads you, no matter what the cost, He will do something beyond your imagination—I promise you.

13. What is one area of your life God is asking you to surrender and trust into His hands?

_____

_____

14. Read Mark 10:29–30. What does Jesus promise to give in this life to those who have made sacrifices to follow Him?

_____

_____

15. Now read Psalm 37:3–6. What do these words promise God will do for us as we delight ourselves in Him and commit our ways to Him?

_____

_____

APPLICATION QUESTIONS
. . . .

Read through the following questions and prayerfully answer. Ask the Lord to guide you and speak to your heart.

1. Has God ever invited you into a season of trust and surrender in an area of your life? What happened?

   _____

   _____

2. Why do you think God uses seasons of brokenness to strengthen and develop our relationship with Him?

   _____

   _____

3. Read Philippians 2:3–11. What attitudes did Jesus exemplify and what can we learn from this passage?

   _____

   _____

4. Rephrase in your own words what you think Jesus meant when he said to carry your cross (Luke 14:27).

_____

_____

5. How would you describe the connection between our level of faith and expectations of God?

_____

_____

6. From what you've read in this chapter, explain the importance of our attitudes upon the direction of our lives.

_____

_____

7. What is one area God has spoken to you about through this chapter? How will you respond to Him?

_____

_____

Chapter 3
DEVOTION

I am saying this for your own good ... that you may live in a right way in undivided devotion to the Lord.
—1 Corinthians 7:35

I didn't realize how bad I felt internally when I was heavier, unfit, and unhealthy. But now that I'm finally becoming fit and stronger, and eating healthier, I realize how much worse I feel when I step out of that. Nowadays I'm not drinking soda, but whenever I do and drink too much, I feel terrible. Or if I eat at McDonald's because I'm in a hurry or something, about an hour later I feel like road kill.

These experiences have served to shine light on my spiritual life. They made me reflect on the idea of staying spiritually fit. For example, when you're wallowing in sin or not praying, you don't realize at the time how spiritually unhealthy you are. I have come to understand that to see the truth about yourself, you have to walk according to the line God created for you.

I believe it's God's will for us to be fit. He created our bodies to be healthy, and not being healthy is stepping outside of that. *Is that a sin? I think it is for me because I'm addicted to food. I love to eat; it's no secret. If I let myself, I would get very lazy. Therefore for me, I believe that allowing myself to overindulge is a sin.*

In that sense, becoming physically fit has helped my walk with God. It has shown me the importance of being diligent and devoted in the small things. For instance, if I skip my short runs during the week, my long runs on the weekend would be absolutely horrible. Or if I don't drink enough water, don't eat enough of the right kinds of food, or eat whatever I feel like throughout the week, my long runs would be awful. However, those weeks where I do keep up with my runs and water intake, and where I eat vegetables and healthy food, I can finish my longer runs like a hummingbird: All right, let's do another twenty miles! The experience has showed me the value of being faithful in the small things, both physically and in my spiritual life.

I now realize that when the storms come it's important to have been diligent in the small things. In the midst of day-to-day life, I might not see the small matters as all that important, because at the time they don't look that big. Nevertheless anything as simple as just staying diligent in my devotions, praying, and being thankful for what I've got go a long way when the big things come. Staying fit and healthy really do matter.

Jacob

CLOSE ENCOUNTERS OF THE DIVINE KIND

We love because he first loved us.
—1 John 4:19

We're all familiar with the greatest commandment God has given to us: to love the Lord our God with all our heart, soul, mind, and strength (Mark 12:30). But just *how* does one love God? What needs to happen for us to get there? In this chapter we're going to look at the second aspect of our training program: *devotion,* and the keys to growing in love for God and His kingdom purposes.

According to 1 John 4:19, we come to love God as we appreciate how much He loves us and how good He is. Think about it: how can you love someone you hardly know? Experience shows that you grow to love someone as you go through life with that person, witnessing firsthand his or her kindness and generosity toward you. Relationship develops and bonds deepen over time and experience. People generally don't fall in love, real love, with strangers they know nothing about. Rather, we grow in real, lasting love for others through life's events and experiences lived together. This same truth carries over into our relationship with God. As you begin to understand how much He loves you and see expressions of that in your life, your love for Him begins to develop.

Know God's Love

See how very much our Father loves us, for he calls us his children, and that is what we are!
—1 John 3:1, NLT

93

You need to know one very important thing as you embark on developing a deeper relationship with God: He loves you. He truly and deeply loves you simply because you are His child, and He feels all the parental concern and devotion as any good Father does. Yet I know that many people, perhaps even some reading these lines right now, are not convinced of God's love for them.

So let me ask you, how do *you* show your love to someone? Isn't it true that for someone to understand and appreciate that they are loved, they usually need to see it displayed in some way, whether through loving actions or words of some kind? People show and express love in a variety of ways. Some feel loved when they receive a gift, others enjoy receiving messages of encouragement, while still others like to spend time with those they love. We all understand we are loved when we see it displayed in some way. Whatever the demonstration, expressions of love convince us that someone truly loves us.

In the same way, God our heavenly Father has been busy demonstrating His love to us: *"But God showed his great love for us by sending Christ to die for us while we were still sinners* (Romans 5:8, NLT). As this verse reveals, when God gave His Son, Jesus Christ, to die in our place on the cross, He was actually trying to express just how much He loves us. Alan Keiran describes it like this:

> Love motivated [Jesus] to die so you may live forever with Him in heaven. "Greater love has no one than this, that he lay down his life for his friends" (John 15:13). Jesus suffered the humiliation of rejection,

denial, beating, whipping, kicking, spitting, mocking, nakedness, exhaustion, crucifixion, and thirst until He finally gave up His Spirit after six torturous hours on the cross. At any time He could have called for legions of angels to free Him. Instead, He chose the bitter road of humiliation and death so you could experience His unmerited gift of salvation. *Agape* [selfless love] led Jesus to the cross. *Agape* kept Jesus on the cross. *Your Savior loves you that much.*[1]

Giving one's own life on our behalf is the greatest expression of love anyone could ever make, and Jesus has already done this for you. Indeed, God's love was demonstrated again and again whenever Christ touched lepers when no one else would, forgave sinners whom others wanted to condemn, healed the poor and discriminated, and loved the unlovely. Jesus rejected no one and welcomed everyone who wanted to know Him. Friend, God hasn't changed. He still loves His children in these and many other ways. That includes you: "May you experience the love of Christ, though it is too great to understand fully. Then you will be made complete" (Ephesians 3:19, NLT).

As you experience the love of God for yourself and see Him moving in your life, answering your prayers and seeing His good character, you will begin to understand how much He really loves you and, as a result, you will fall in love with your faithful and wonderful God. These expressions of God's love become testimonies of God's love and power in our lives—milestones, if you like, in our relationship with Him.

The Power of Testimonies

You shall diligently keep the commandments of
the Lord your God, and his testimonies and his
statutes, which he has commanded you.
—Deuteronomy 6:17, ESV

Some of the driest Christian circles I've been in are those in which people know much about God in their heads but know Him and His love little in their hearts. If you asked them to share some experience of God from their lives, testimonies when they just *knew* God really answered their prayers in some way, they would struggle to answer. It's as if they are walking with one healthy, muscular leg (Biblical knowledge) and one weak, atrophied leg (experience of God). How sad. This imbalanced knowledge of God makes it impossible to run as God intends.

Yet testimonies are powerful and necessary in our lives, which is why God commanded the Israelites to not only teach their children the commands of God but also the testimonies of God's miracles (see Deuteronomy 6). Beloved, God does not want you to have a dry, Christian experience. Rather, He desires that you encounter Him and His expressions of love in your everyday life. Too many believers do not realize God wants to speak into their lives and reveal Himself to them. As we begin to experience God in such powerful ways, we create testimonial milestones in our lives, which we can later look back on and encourage ourselves with. Those precious seasons in life that we have come through together with God build and bolster our faith enormously, and they are one of the main ways we grow in our love and devotion for Him.

Devotion

Past testimonies create faith in God for the present.

The psalmists understood the power of encountering God in real ways and often looked back at what God had done to encourage them in their current circumstances:

> Has his unfailing love vanished forever? Has his promise failed for all time? Has God forgotten to be merciful? Has he in anger withheld his compassion? Then I thought, "To this I will appeal: the years of the right hand of the Most High." I will remember the deeds of the Lord; yes, I will remember your miracles of long ago. I will meditate on all your works and consider all your mighty deeds (Psalm 77:8–12).

The writer was clearly depressed and discouraged. Just as we do at times, he questioned if God still loved him and whether He was angry with him. In spite of how he felt, he made a deliberate faith decision to look back and meditate upon the miracles and mighty deeds he knew God had done in the past. Those milestones served to encourage him and lift him out of his pit of hopelessness.

The Bible clearly speaks of the influence of God's work and miracles in our lives to strengthen our faith and obedience. In the New Testament we read the account of Jesus turning water into wine and what this miracle did in the hearts of those who witnessed it: "This, the first of his miraculous signs, Jesus performed in Cana of Galilee. He thus revealed his glory, and his disciples put their faith in him" (John

2:11). This miracle served to create faith in the hearts of His disciples, faith that encouraged them to follow Christ.

After His ascension, Jesus Christ continued His work of drawing people to Himself through the words and actions of His disciples: "So Paul and Barnabas spent considerable time there, speaking boldly for the Lord, who confirmed the message of his grace by enabling them to do miraculous signs and wonders" (Acts 14:3).

In both the Old and New Testaments, signs and miracles not only met the felt needs of individuals but fostered faith in God, drawing people to Him in love and obedience. Why should His way of working be any different today?

We serve a God who hasn't changed. He still loves to reveal Himself and speak with His people according to their needs. The Bible is full of testimonies of God communicating with people and miraculously intervening in their lives. It is completely Biblical to expect divine encounters in your life. My friend, you should believe God for more.

1. Read Mark 8:1–21. What point do you think Jesus was trying to make through His questions to His disciples in verses 17–21?

2. Why is it important that we understand and meditate on the miracles and answers to prayer we've experienced for our future faith walk?

_____

_____

3. According to John 13:34, what enables us to love one another? What have been some moments when you have felt most loved by God?

_____

_____

LIVING BY THE SPIRIT

And when you believed in Christ, he identified you as his own by giving you the Holy Spirit, whom he promised long ago. The Spirit is God's guarantee that he will give us the inheritance he promised and that he has purchased us to be his own people.
—Ephesians 1:13–14, NLT

God gives His Holy Spirit to empower us as witnesses of Jesus Christ and to act as a guarantee of our salvation. Receiving and living by the Holy Spirit was considered a mark of true discipleship by the early disciples.

Too many believers today have confused living by the Spirit with living by their feelings. In other words, we think our feelings are an accurate judge of the will of God, and so we make important decisions in relationships, church life, work, and so on depending on how we *feel* at a particular moment.

Friend, living by our emotions and living by the Spirit are not one and the same. Our feelings can change from moment to moment and are not reliable guides. Living by our feelings is merely a carnal form of Christianity, and that is not how God wants you to live.

If you really desire the relationship with God you've always wanted, you need to learn how to be led by the Spirit. Now don't get nervous. I'm not about to dive off the charismatic deep end. I'm simply talking about learning to live by the Spirit as the Bible teaches. God longs for you to learn how to live by His Spirit to guide and direct you, comfort and strengthen you, equip and empower you into God's will and purposes for your life.

The Seal of Discipleship

I will ask the Father, and he will give you another Counselor to be with you forever—the Spirit of truth. ... You know him, for he lives with you and will be in you. I will not leave you as orphans; I will come to you.
—John 14:16–18

Before He ascended to the Father, Jesus explained that He was not going to leave His disciples alone but that He would send His Spirit to take His place. Later, in John 16, Jesus went even further by saying the presence of the Spirit in their lives would be better than having Him in the flesh (verse 7). What a statement! He knew the Spirit's presence was absolutely vital for their life and witness. Indeed, it was this filling of God's Spirit that enabled those fearful, doubting disciples to transform into anointed witnesses of the risen Jesus Christ (Acts 2).

In the same way, because we are children of God, disciples of Jesus Christ, we can ask God to fill us with His Holy Spirit. We also need God's living presence in our lives. Just as the early church considered living by the Spirit as a mark of real discipleship, we too can learn what it means to live by the Spirit and be transformed from fearful followers to empowered disciples of the living Christ: "Having believed, you were marked in him with a seal, the promised Holy Spirit, who is a deposit guaranteeing our inheritance (Ephesians 1:13–14).

Following God is more than just enjoying His peace and guidance. It's about walking with and experiencing Him day by day: hearing His voice, recognizing and following His promptings, knowing His guidance, experiencing His love and power. As Ephesians 3:20 promises, God is able to do for us far more than all we can imagine because He loves us and His power is at work in our lives.

How then can we learn to live by the Spirit and receive from God all He desires to give us? How can we grow in our relationship with God as we long for?

How Spiritual Growth Happens

Despite the readily available presence and ministry of the Holy Spirit, many who profess to be Christians are ignorant of His work. Sadly, they are not living the empowered and effective Christian life God desires for them.

In their book, *Move: What 1,000 Churches Reveal about Spiritual Growth*, Greg L. Hawkins and Cally Parkinson describe the shock the leadership team of Willow Creek Church in Chicago experienced after reading the results of a congregational survey they conducted on the spiritual condition of their members. Among their findings they discovered,

- Church activities do not predict or drive long-term spiritual growth.
- Lots of apathetic nonbelievers who attend church are unlikely to ever accept Christ.
- Spiritually stalled or dissatisfied people account for one out of four church congregants (in some churches the percentage was as high as 50 percent).[2]

Pastor of Willow Creek Church, Bill Hybels, writes:

What they discovered challenged some of our core assumptions about our effectiveness as a church. For example, 18 percent of our congregation—more than 1,000 people—had stalled spiritually and didn't know what to do about it. Many were considering leaving. And some of our most mature and fired-up Christians wanted to go deeper in their faith and be challenged more but felt as if our church wasn't helping them get to the next level.[3]

After expanding their survey to include 250,000 congregation members from one-thousand other churches nationwide for more than four years, they were surprised to find similar results. They concluded that true spiritual growth wasn't determined by a person's involvement in church activities. A person could be involved for many years in a church ministry without growing significantly. They discovered the most effective strategy for enabling people to progress in their faith was their level of *Biblical engagement* in their everyday lives. In other words, people grew spiritually by learning to hear from God and encountering Him by living out His Word.

Word and Spirit

How we respond to the Scriptures has everything to do with our spiritual quality of life. Look at those two words again: *Biblical engagement*. That's not the same as just reading the Bible. Many Christians read the Bible and are still spiritually stalled and lifeless. The members of Willow Creek Church had heard great sermons every weekend and spent time reading the Bible. Biblical engagement goes a step further: it involves both reading *and* applying God's Word. As you learn how to live out and apply God's Word, you begin to discern the voice and leading of God's Spirit and you begin to see God fulfill His wonderful promises. That's when you see the power of God at work. The following simple diagram explains how that happens:

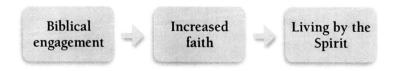

| Biblical engagement | ⇒ | Increased faith | ⇒ | Living by the Spirit |

This is crucial for your spiritual growth: *Biblical engagement leads to increased faith, which in turn enables you to live by the Spirit.* As Romans 10:17 says, "So faith comes from hearing, and hearing through the Word of Christ" (ESV). If you want to overcome spiritual stagnation and see your faith grow, then it begins with immersing yourself in the Word of God and applying it. As you begin to apply God's Word, your faith in turn grows, and in turn, your faith enables you to live by the Spirit.

Think about it: how can we follow the promptings of God's Spirit without faith? It won't happen. Sure, we may understand what God is saying, but without faith, we will never have the courage to follow through. That's why you need faith to live by the Spirit, and faith comes from applying the Word of God.

There are no shortcuts, my friend. If you want more faith, you must believe and apply God's Word, and in turn, you will find yourself empowered to live by the Spirit. Biblical engagement, then, is fundamental to spiritual growth, for this is where encountering God and falling in love with Him begins. Everything you need to know about God—His character and will, His love for you, His wonderful promises, the power of prayer, His purposes, and so much more—are found in the Holy Scriptures.

God moves in response to active (not passive) faith. Therefore it follows that to see God move in your life, you start by believing *and* living like you believe the promises of God. It's not rocket science, nor is it too mysterious for us to understand. God has provided many promises for us in His written Word on subjects including guidance, practical provision, healing, strength, and so on. It's as you take God's promises seriously and stand on His Word in those tough seasons of life that your faith will grow and you will experience God's faithfulness for yourself.

Spirit-Filled Discipleship

As you exercise faith in God's Word, your faith releases the power of God. Jesus referred to this spiritual principle in Mark 11:24: your active faith in God's Word will release God's power so you can encounter God. Live by faith in God's Word and you will begin to see God working in your life. There are many different kinds of ways we can see and encounter God in our lives including:

- *Hearing God speak to us*—through a variety of ways including Scripture (primary means, of course), dreams, a picture or impression coming to mind, a prophetic word, or even the actual gentle voice of the Holy Spirit speaking directly to us (Keep in mind that God will never contradict His written Word)
- *Receiving specific answers to prayer*—including miraculous provision, protection, healing, guidance or other divine intervention
- *Strong sense of God's presence*—bringing comfort when in distress or confidence that God has heard your prayer

I love God's Word and it's the basis upon which I live my life. I believe God's Word is completely true and that God is utterly faithful to His promises. From the very beginning of my walk with God, I have experienced God's guidance as I choose to take Him at His Word.

When I first decided to follow God at seventeen years of age, having had no religious background, I had a simple, perhaps naïve, faith in God's Word. If it said it, I believed it. I remember in the first month of my new walk as I was learning how to pray, words came to my mind that I had never heard of. I realized that perhaps those words were in the Bible, so I turned to the contents page and discovered it was the name of a book in the Bible. God had impressed this specific passage, including chapter reference, on my mind to speak to me. I was amazed God would speak to someone like me who had absolutely no knowledge of Scripture. This happened on two separate occasions, and each time the different passages spoke about the same particular sin. That first encounter with God showed me not only my sin but that He was real after all, a testimony I have never forgotten and which in turn, moved me to seriously seek after God.

Almost twenty-five years later, I am still encountering God through His Word and by His Spirit, though as the years go by, in additional ways. Sometimes God wakes me up in the night leading me to pray for someone. On occasions He shows me someone's specific need in my dreams. I've also experienced God by hearing His Spirit gently speaking to me—through a Bible passage or a specific revelation—for the encouragement of others or myself. I have experienced

God healing me physically and emotionally, impressing important events upon me just before they actually happen to warn and prepare me, and protecting me in spiritual warfare. The list could go on. But it all begins with immersing myself in God's Word and believing it.

God gives us His Spirit so we may live the Christian life He desires for us. Whenever I think about how God has revealed Himself to me and worked in my life, I find that my love and appreciation for Him greatly deepens. You will find that too. Active faith in His written Word and His Holy Spirit form a powerful partnership. As you immerse yourself in His Word and prayer, you will come to understand His will and character and learn how to recognize His voice.

Whenever God reveals something through His Word or speaks by His Spirit, don't doubt it. Doubt never does anyone any good, nor does God promise any reward for doubt. God's words are precious and flawless and can be completely believed: "The words of the Lord are pure words, like silver refined in a furnace on the ground, purified seven times" (Psalm 12:6, ESV).

I encourage you to begin the very good habit of keeping a journal to regularly write down what God teaches you or reveals to you. I find that looking back on God's revelations and testimonies provides great strength and encouragement through the tougher seasons of life.

God is faithful to His Word and if you are willing to believe what He says, you too will encounter God through His Spirit as you stand on His promises. Your life will never be the same.

4. Read Galatians 5:16–26. What are the two ways of living according to this passage? What is the fruit of living by God's Spirit?

_____

_____

5. According to verse 24, if we belong to Christ Jesus, what have we done?

_____

_____

6. Have you experienced God speaking to you through the Bible? If so, how?

_____

_____

DOING THE WORKS OF JESUS

Seek the Kingdom of God above all else, and live righteously, and he will give you everything you need.
—Matthew 6:33, NLT

So far in this chapter we've looked at how love and devotion for God develops in our lives: through encountering and experiencing God. We've also seen what it means to live by God's Word and Spirit. In this next section, I want to look at why God gives us His Spirit and what it means to fulfill God's purposes in our lives.

Ambitious for God's Glory

God is looking for ambitious children. I'm not talking about ambition in the material sense but a burning ambition for His name and glory here on earth. One great example of this is seen in the life of the late Christian sprinter, Eric Liddell.

Liddell was very ambitious for God. The movie about his life, *Chariots of Fire*, relates the true story of his refusal to run in a Sunday race in the 1924 Olympic Games in Paris. He would not go against his religious convictions by running on a Sunday and ended up withdrawing from the 100-meter race, his best event. Even though it seemed he was being foolish and all hopes of an Olympic medal were dashed, he adamantly refused to put his running before God.

Later that week, a fellow team member unexpectedly gave up his place in the 400-meter so Liddell could run. Although he hadn't trained for that distance, Liddell did run and God honored his obedience. He came away from those Olympics with a gold medal. John W. Keddie wrote of Liddell:

> Eric was always wholehearted in what he did, whether in student evangelism, studies or sport. He was a good role model for young people for dedication and determination in the tasks he undertook. He was,

of course, concerned that God would be honoured by what he did and said.

He never prayed that he would win the Olympic events, or any other event for that matter. He recognized that would be simply selfish and unworthy. He did pray, however, that in the meetings, as in all else in his life, the Lord would be glorified, and that He might be pleased to use Eric's witness for his Lord to the blessing of others.[4]

Successful athletes are ambitious. They have a specific purpose and goal that drive what they do. Yet how ambitious are we for God and His kingdom? How driven are we as spiritual athletes to promoting His name? We don't like to talk about being ambitious—it might sound as if we're being proud—yet plenty of people in this world are way more ambitious for the sake of their religions than we are. Friend, holding back from being ambitious for God only hinders God's kingdom purposes from being accomplished here on earth. God wants you to shine for Him and His glory.

Created for a Purpose

For we are God's workmanship, created in Christ Jesus to do good works, which God prepared in advance for us to do.
—Ephesians 2:10

Whoever we are and whatever our backgrounds, creeds, or culture, we all have an inbuilt longing to live for meaning and a worthy purpose in life. Anyone who fails to find purpose can easily fall into depression. It's a basic human fact that we all need hope and we all need purpose.

According to Ephesians 2:10, you have been created for a very specific purpose: to do good works that God has already preordained for you to do. Just take that in for a moment. You have been created in Christ Jesus to do good works. Not just any kind of work, but God's work, which is good. What exactly does that look like? Take a look at Jesus' words:

> Believe me that I am in the Father and the Father is in me, or else believe on account of the *works* themselves. Truly, truly, I say to you, *whoever* believes in me will also do the *works* that I do; and greater *works* than these will he do, because I am going to the Father. Whatever you ask in my name, this I will do, that the Father may be glorified in the Son. If you ask me anything in my name, I will do it (John 14:11–14, ESV, emphasis added).

These words of Christ have the power to transform lives. Listen carefully to what Jesus is saying: anyone who believes in Him will continue to do the wonderful works He did. Let me unwrap this.

The English word translated as *works* in Ephesians 2:10 is the same word in the original Greek as the word translated *works* found here. Do you realize what this means? The good works you've been created to do are the same works Jesus Himself did here on earth. In fact, according to Jesus, He has called us to do greater works! All for the purpose of God's glory.

What is that work? Jesus described it clearly in Luke 4:18: "The Spirit of the Lord is on me, because he has anointed me to preach good news to the poor. He has sent me to proclaim freedom for the prisoners and recovery of sight for the blind, to release the oppressed."

I'm not telling you to go out and buy a long robe and sandals and start looking for people being lowered from ceilings or climbing trees. But I am saying that God wants to use you to bring hope and healing into the lives of those around you, obeying the second greatest commandment, to love your neighbor (Matthew 22:38). Whether you're a full-time parent, office worker, lawyer, business executive, CEO, financial adviser, truck driver, pastor, student, or job seeker, myriads of people in your life need God and what He has to offer: salvation, freedom from life-sapping addictions, healing in marriages and other relationships, physical healing, purpose in life, and so on. God is still in the business of saving and healing people's lives, and He wants to use *you* as a channel of His good work.

You are a channel of God's kingdom purposes.

As you believe God's Word and follow the promptings of the Spirit living in you, God will use you to reveal Him and His love to those He puts you in contact with. You have a wonderful purpose in life, and if you are willing you can be part of the most exciting adventure of your life: "Jesus Christ, who gave himself for us to redeem us from all lawlessness and to purify for himself a people for his own possession who are zealous for good *works* (Titus 2:13–14, ESV, emphasis added). Yes, it is the same word again.

I hope it's becoming clear. You have been saved for a purpose: to do the good works God has preordained and prepared for you, the same works Jesus did. Your life is no accident. God has uniquely created you, just the way you are, with your unique talents, strengths, and spiritual gifts, which equip you to serve Him. You are alive for a purpose: to do good works.

Rely on God's Resources

I'm sure you're probably wondering, *How can I possibly do the works Jesus did? I'm not the Son of God!* True, but you are a child of God. The good news is that God does not ask you to fulfill His purposes in your strength and ability alone. Rather, just as Christ empowered His disciples in the Upper Room in Acts 2 through the filling of His Spirit, so God has empowered you. You have the Spirit of Christ living in you and therefore have more resources and power at your disposal than you realize:

> I keep asking that the God of our Lord Jesus Christ, the glorious Father, may give you the Spirit of wisdom and revelation, so that you may know him better. I pray also that the eyes of your heart may be enlightened in order that you may know … his incomparably great power for us who believe. That power is like the working of his mighty strength,

which he exerted in Christ when he raised him from the dead (Ephesians 1:17–20).

These believers in Ephesus were in the same boat as many of us: they didn't understand the power of God available to them to live as witnesses of Christ. That's why the apostle Paul prayed for them, that God would open their eyes to see their incomparably great power. You too have this same power. Everything you need to do God's work will be given to you: "And God is able to make all grace abound to you, so that in all things at all times, having all that you need, you will abound in every good work" (2 Corinthians 9:8).

As Ephesians 2:10 declares, you are God's workmanship, created to do God's good works, which He has already prepared in advance for you to do. Whatever you need to do His work—finances, strength, wisdom, health, power, opportunities, partners, or guidance—God promises to supply. As you seek God and His kingdom first, you will see God working in you and through you in wonderful ways. Not only that, but you will find yourself falling in love with your wonderful Creator more and more.

I humbly invite you to become ambitious for God's glory, for as Liddell discovered, those who live for God's glory will be rewarded. You cannot outgive God, who desires to use your life to bring Him great glory in the eyes of an unbelieving world. Child of God, rise up and let God use you for His kingdom purposes. Shine for His glory.

7. Has God placed a particular dream or ambition in your heart? If yes, what is it? Pray and ask God to prepare you and open doors for that to happen.

_____

_____

_____

8. Read 1 Corinthians 12. How does this chapter apply to your life?

_____

_____

_____

9. Pray and ask the Lord to expand your ambition and desire for Him and the advancement of His kingdom where you live.

_____

_____

_____

GOING FOR GOLD

*In a large house there are articles not only of gold and silver,
but also of wood and clay; some are for noble purposes and
some for ignoble. If a man cleanses himself of the latter,
he will be an instrument for noble purposes, made holy,
useful to the Master and prepared to do any good work.*
—2 Timothy 2:20–21

One of my favorite series of books is *God's Generals* by Roberts Liardon. In his many books, he describes the lives, struggles and accomplishments of many of the great Christian men and women from the past: Kathryn Kuhlman, Jonathan Edwards, Charles Finney, George Mueller, John G. Lake, William and Catherine Booth, and so on.[5]

Those great men and women of faith were instruments of noble purposes used by God to bring His kingdom here on earth. They were totally devoted to God and the advancement of His kingdom, men and women whom God used to bring the gospel of Jesus Christ to many millions around the world, seeing countless healed of various sicknesses. Whenever I read about the lives of such people, I am greatly inspired and invigorated to run and seek after God just as they did. They gave God everything they had and saw God move in amazing ways as a result. They were going for gold for God.

Oh, how we can learn from their passion and unrelenting devotion. The amazing truth is that you too can be an instrument of gold, used by God for His noble purposes. Whoever you are, whatever your background, God can use you, for it's not the wise and learned that God often chooses to use, but those who are unheard of, without reputation, and unknown:

> Brothers, think of what you were when you were called. Not many of you were wise by human standards; not many were influential; not many were of noble birth. But God chose the foolish things of the world to shame the wise; God chose the weak things of the world to shame the strong. He chose the lowly things of this world and the despised things—and the things that are not—to nullify the things that are, so that no one may boast before him (1 Corinthians 1:26–29).

The only criterion God requires is a humble heart of faith and obedience. He does the rest. I love what inspirational speaker and author, Nick Vujicic, writes on the value of living wholeheartedly for God and His purpose:

> The late Helen Keller lost her sight and hearing before the age of two due to illness, but she went on to become a world-renowned author, speaker, and social activist. This great woman said true happiness comes through "fidelity to a worthy purpose." What does that mean? For me, it means being faithful to your gifts, growing them, sharing them, and taking joy in them. It means moving beyond the pursuit of self-satisfaction to the more mature search for meaning and fulfillment. The greatest rewards come

when you give of yourself. It's about bettering the lives of others, being part of something bigger than you, and making a positive difference. You don't have to be Mother Teresa to do that. You can even be a "disabled" guy and make an impact.[6]

Nick Vujicic is an amazing instrument of God. He travels the world as an inspirational speaker, yet you may be surprised to hear he was born with no arms or legs. Despite his disability, he realized after a very difficult period in his life that God had gifted him in other ways. Now he spends much time traveling around the world, bringing a message of hope and faith to thousands of adults and young people. Nick Vujicic doesn't focus on what he doesn't have; he looks at what God *has* given him and to the purpose God has called him to fulfill, and he is passionately and wholeheartedly doing that. God is using Nick to touch and transform *so* many lives because he is devoted to living for God's purpose and passionately loving every minute of it. He is truly running for gold as a spiritual athlete.

There is no reason why you cannot become an instrument like these great men and women of God, past and present. The only thing holding you back is *you*. Don't let a lack of confidence or faith or even willingness stop you from running with God. God is able to give you whatever you need if you ask Him. How you build here on earth brings lasting results:

If any man builds on this foundation using gold, silver, costly stones, wood, hay or straw, his work will be shown for what it is, because the Day will bring it to light. It will be revealed with fire, and the fire will test the quality of each man's work. If what he has built survives, he will receive his reward. If it is burned up, he will suffer loss; he himself will be saved, but only as one escaping through the flames (1 Corinthians 3:12–15).

I don't know about you, but I want my work to pass the test of fire. I want to build as best as I can with God's help and strength. I want to receive a reward from my Master when the Day comes. Don't you?

10. Is there a man or woman of God, past or present, whom you admire? What inspires you about this person?

_____

_____

11. How did *you* first come to know Christ? Share that story.

_____

_____

12. Is there any real reason you cannot become all God desires you to be? Pray about that.

POWER, LOVE, AND SELF-DISCIPLINE

For God did not give us a spirit of timidity, but a spirit of power, of love and of self-discipline.
—2 Timothy 1:7

Ask any group of athletes how they accomplished their goals and dreams and they will tell you it took a whole lot of discipline and dedication. They will explain how there were days when they didn't feel like doing another circuit or swimming another lap or sticking to their diet. Yet despite how they felt, they willfully chose to continually put in the effort and discipline because they badly wanted to succeed.

We may be tempted to think that becoming mature in our relationship with God and having the relationship with God we've always desired will come through occasional eruptions of effort, but from my own experience and that of millions around the world, that's not the way spiritual muscle develops. Imagine if a boxer worked out only when he felt like it, or if a gymnast frequented the gym only when she thought she had time. I'm sure they wouldn't get very far despite their desires and great ambitions. Good intentions are not enough, for spiritual development will only come as you put in the regular effort and discipline. Orlick describes its importance:

> All people have the capacity to excel, or become the best they can be, at something. To turn your capacity into a living reality, you have to make the decision to focus fully on doing it. You have to choose to pour your heart and soul into it. It is that simple. And it is totally within your control. When you make the decision to do something with commitment and quality, all the rest is focus. How far your journey takes you depends on the depth and direction of your focus.[7]

Orlick has coached and instructed the best in the sports world, Olympic champions and the like, and he has found that giving your dream your heart and soul are absolutely essential for success.

Exercise Discipline

> *So think clearly and exercise self-control.*
> —1 Peter 1:13, NLT

If exercising self-discipline and self-control were not possible, I'm sure Paul would have excluded it from 2 Timothy 1:7. Yet he didn't. Why? Because God's Spirit who lives in us provides us with the power, love, *and* self-discipline we need as followers of Christ. You already have everything you need available to you. You just need to believe it and act on it.

To grow and become stronger as a disciple of Jesus Christ you will need to tap into the self-discipline God has already provided. No one finds exercising self-discipline easy; it always requires effort and the exercise of one's volition. Yet the more you exercise it, the easier it becomes over time.

DISCIPLINE REAPS REWARD

Begin, as every athlete does, by figuring out which area you need to develop. Think clearly about where you desire to improve, and create some goals toward that. So, for example, perhaps you desire to develop your prayer life or become more confident in trusting God. These kind of goals, as 1 Peter 1:13 teaches us, will require us to exercise effort and discipline in our behavior that will enable that to happen.

One man in the Bible who understood the need for daily discipline and focus was King David. He knew developing his relationship with God wouldn't just happen by itself; he would have to devote himself to spending time to his pursuit of God. He wrote in Psalm 1,

> Blessed is the man who does not walk in the counsel of the wicked or stand in the way of sinners or sit in the seat of mockers. But his delight is in the law of the Lord, and on his law he meditates day and night. He is like a tree planted by streams of water, which yields its fruit in season and whose leaf does not wither. Whatever he does prospers (vv. 1–3).

David was a disciplined man who loved God and wanted more of Him in his life. Knowing and loving God is not simply about what we *feel* about Him. If we truly love God, we will do what He says (John 14:15). How we live is a true reflection of our love for God. If we love God, we will want to please Him and obey Him accordingly. If we don't, we won't. It's that simple. You cannot separate how you live day to day from your love for God.

David concentrated on what he knew would build him up in God: the daily reading of and meditating on God's Word. He knew that to know God and obey Him he needed to bring himself under the influence of God's Word. To do that, he had to discipline himself and set aside the time he needed each day.

It doesn't take long for me to see my faith and relationship with God weaken. All it takes is a few days of neglect and busying myself with other things. That's why at the beginning of my walk with God many years ago, I made the decision to prioritize spending time with Him every day. It doesn't just happen by itself; no, it requires self-discipline, getting up a few hours early to spend time with God in His Word and prayer. Every morning, however busy the day ahead, I get up early and come before God, focusing my mind and heart on Him and His Word, committing the whole day to Him. Also, whenever I get the chance, I look for good Christian books on subjects I'm weak in or ignorant about. Sure, it costs money and time, but it's an investment that is worth it. As a result, I am greatly encouraged when I see my relationship with God grow and my understanding of spiritual things deepen. But it takes deliberate discipline every day to see the fruit.

Understand that real growth involves all three: power, love, and self-discipline, and thankfully God has already equipped you with these through His Spirit. If you find yourself being pulled away from running after God by other demanding responsibilities, then it's time to exercise discipline. Sometimes we have to say no, either to ourselves and how we're feeling or to others and their burdens upon our time. To love God with all our heart, soul, mind, and strength is the first and greatest commandment and priority we have as believers. Don't allow anything to get in the way.

13. Why do you think exercising self-discipline is important as a disciple? How does 2 Timothy 1:7 apply to you?

_____

_____

14. Can you remember a time when you felt particular love and devotion for God? What caused that?

_____

15. Do you think your obedience to God should be controlled by how you feel? Why or why not?

_____

_____

APPLICATION QUESTIONS

Read through and prayerfully answer the following questions. Ask the Lord to guide you and speak to your heart.

1. Why do you think compromise in your relationship with God prevents you from experiencing His power?

    _____

    _____

2. Read John 14:12–14. What does Jesus promise for anyone who believes in Him?

    _____

    _____

3. Read 1 Corinthians 12. According to verse 7, why does God entrust us with spiritual gifts?

    _____

    _____

Devotion

4. How many spiritual gifts can you identify in this chapter? Do you know what your gifts are?

_____

_____

5. Read 2 Timothy 2:20–21. According to these verses, how can we prepare ourselves for God's work?

_____

_____

6. What does a life look like that is fully surrendered to God's plan? Are you surrendered to God's plans for you?

_____

_____

7. What is one area God has spoken to you about through this chapter? How will you respond to Him?

_____

_____

PART TWO

GET SET

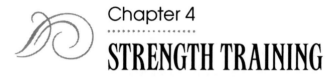

Chapter 4

STRENGTH TRAINING

I discipline my body like an athlete, training it to do what it should. Otherwise, I fear that after preaching to others I myself might be disqualified.
—1 Corinthians 9:27, NLT

When I decided to run a marathon, I wasn't a runner; I didn't even enjoy running! I had always been into fitness, so I can't say I was physically unfit. But running was always unpleasant for me, unless I was chasing a ball or chasing somebody while playing a sport. The idea came up because it was a challenge and it seemed like something that would build a routine that I did not otherwise have for fitness in my life.

So I started a four-month training program, and the first thing I did was ask people around me if they would do it with me. I knew I wouldn't keep myself accountable if I tried to do it by myself. I successfully managed to get one friend to do it with me, which was great.

We started our training program at a very foundational level: three miles of running. So it wasn't like we had to do much to get started. When we first started, we were excited. We were intimidated by the idea of doing a marathon, but we knew this training program had been put together by runners who had successfully completed the same plan. OK, we thought, if other people did it, we can, too. We've got four months. They're telling us we've got enough time. We're just going to do what they say because we don't know what we're doing. We simply committed to following the plan.

The first training session we did together was six miles, the longest either of us had ever run. So that itself was a huge accomplishment. We were saying to ourselves, that was so easy! We were talking the whole time about what we hoped to accomplish and were excited about the process of preparing for the marathon. We talked about nutrition, weight-loss goals, and other things like that.

The plan we were on was basic: We had one long run each week, and for that we would really push ourselves for distance. Then, on the other four days, we were running shorter distances; the longest of which was eight miles. The remaining two days were mandatory rest, which was very important.

At the beginning, the biggest thing that stood out to me was the feeling of success in the little runs. I thought it was strange that they had us doing so many short runs. I sometimes thought, We should be working on distance. We should be trying to do these really long runs all the time. Why are we doing all these short runs? But we found that the short runs helped us feel accomplished and they got us used to the idea of running all the time.

I realized the huge parallel with spirituality when I was running. We all have these big spiritual goals we want to accomplish. But actually, it's the small ones, all the little things we do, that count the most. To accomplish something great, you simply have to start small.

Megan

GETTING STARTED

Do you not know that in a race all the runners run,
but only one gets the prize? Run in such a way as to
get the prize. Everyone who competes in the games
goes into strict training. They do it to get a crown that
will not last; but we do it to get a crown that will last
forever. Therefore I do not run like a man running
aimlessly; I do not fight like a man beating the air.
—1 Corinthians 9:24–26

Athletes put their bodies through rigorous training to achieve a prize that doesn't even last. If athletes train themselves so thoroughly to achieve their temporary material prizes, how much more should we devote ourselves to obtaining lasting, heavenly gain? As the verses above indicate, we become the best athletes we can be through wholehearted, deliberate, and focused effort. Therefore, in this chapter we will look at the next aspect of our training program, *strength training,* and some crucial areas that will enhance our spiritual growth.

The Value of Preparation

In the opening verses of this section, the writer alluded to two different sports, running and boxing, to illustrate the necessity of proper training and decisive direction to succeed in becoming spiritual athletes. Athletes know they cannot afford to play their sports without clear purpose and direction. A boxer doesn't just beat the air and a runner doesn't just run aimlessly. What would be the point of that?

Instead, as Megan learned, they have a plan with goals and specific steps. In other words, athletes don't just run or fight without any thought, simply hoping for the best. They go into "strict training" with step-by-step, specific goals that will ultimately enable them to succeed. Winning won't happen by itself. As with any field of life, winners put their bodies and minds through tough preparation and education. Michael Lardon wrote in *Finding Your Zone, Ten Core Lessons for Achieving Peak Performance in Sports and Life*,

> In business, the people who prepare systematically before a big presentation generally perform their best on the day of the presentation itself. The skill and knowledge that is required to perform well under pressure is not obtained moments before the performance. As with golf or any other sport, you have to be able to take your game from the driving range to the course: Comprehensive preparation takes foresight and is obtained over many weeks, months, or years of dedicated work. When you've accomplished this level of preparation, then your mind is more at ease during times of pressure or stress. Great preparation allows you to lose your worries and simply become one with the task at hand.[1]

In the same way, dedication to a planned training program is absolutely necessary to see spiritual growth. After all, isn't that why Paul alluded to sports in our opening passage? We are often ready to give our best to our careers, making money, or our physical appearance, but not to what has lasting value. Due to our busy lives and desires for other things, God often ends up becoming our last resort or priority. I'm sure you'd agree: that's not running the race well but simply ambling along—and that level of effort never gets anyone very far. Friend, if you want to see God move today in ways you read about in the Bible, if you truly desire a Spirit-led life, then you need to run deliberately and intentionally, and invest into some comprehensive training.

If you are willing to put the time and effort into your personal development, you will achieve real growth, which will also protect you when the storms of life roll in. Consider what Jesus said:

> Therefore everyone who hears these words of mine and puts them into practice is like a wise man who built his house on the rock. The rain came down, the streams rose, and the winds blew and beat against that house; yet it did not fall, because it had its foundation on the rock. But everyone who hears these words of mine and does not put them into practice is like a foolish man who built his house on sand. The rain came down, the streams rose, and the winds blew and beat against that house, and it fell with a great crash (Matthew 7:24–27).

I remember a story I heard by apologist Ravi Zacharias. He and his wife were visiting London soon after bad storms had hit the country. He explained how they saw, in the center of London, hundreds of large trees that had been uprooted by the storms, but he couldn't understand why. Later someone explained to him that although many trees in the U.K. are large, the roots are often shallow. Because of the plentiful supply of rain, roots don't need to go down deep into the soil to find nutrients, so they remain near the surface where there is plenty of nutrition. As a result, when the storms came, these large trees fell because of their shallow roots.

This story and Jesus' parable explain the importance of sending our roots down deep into God's Word. In Matthew 7, Jesus explained how both men had been blessed with the same privilege of hearing the Word of God. Yet each man responded differently: one took His words seriously and put them into practice, but the other didn't. The difference in their resulting ability and strength to survive the storms was stark: one man survived when the hurricane hit while the other was destroyed.

The wise man experienced in a dramatic way the benefits of applying God's Word into his life. As a result of his months and years of spiritual investment, he was strengthened and equipped to survive the storm. He not only listened to the words of God, he took them seriously and applied them to his life. He lived by them, and by choosing that kind of response, he built his life on a solid foundation. The foolish man, however, didn't make the effort to live his life by the words of God, so when the storms hit, he was devastated and eventually lost everything because his roots and foundation were shallow.

Small Steps

As we know, good intentions alone don't get us far. Growing in our knowledge of God and His purpose for our lives can seem like an Everest to climb. However, what at first seems impossible and overwhelming to us can in fact be accomplished by taking small, incremental steps.

The idea of taking baby steps helped me when I realized it was time to finally get fit physically. Suddenly finding myself with time on my hands, I knew I couldn't put it off any longer; otherwise it would probably never happen. Having been a follower of Christ for about twenty-five years, I understood that just as spiritual growth doesn't happen by itself, neither does physical fitness. I realized I needed to decide to commit to getting fit and strong, yet it seemed overwhelming to me.

So I began by focusing on taking small steps. The first need was to purchase the tools necessary: clothing and shoes. I didn't have any sports gear, nor did I know where to buy them in this foreign city where I live. So I prayed and asked God to show me where I could purchase these things (I figured God knew), and He did. He brought to mind a certain floor of a local department store, which I had never visited before, and sure enough, there was all the sports gear I needed. Isn't God clever?

My next step required more of a commitment: getting in the car and driving to my local gym to find out what exercise classes they offered. This felt more serious and took courage. I felt intimidated walking into a sports center with lots of physically fit people walking around. Yet I knew I had to bite the bullet and go find out. I knew attending a fitness class with a structured program would help me stay committed and motivated, which turned out to be the case.

The hardest part in the whole process, though, especially at the beginning, was getting up early and going to the classes. I didn't know anyone or anything about the class, but I knew I *had* to go and trust God if I wanted to accomplish my goal to get healthy. I started with easier classes, not pushing myself too hard, giving my body time to adjust to the shock of exercise. I did try running on the treadmill, but I quickly realized my body was nowhere near ready for that. So I bought a rowing machine and later changed to an exercise bike and worked on these at home several times a week. All in all, I allocated times in my schedule that I thought would be enough to reach my goals, just taking little steps, one at a time. To my great delight and amazement, as the weeks and months went by, I saw the weight slowly begin to fall off and muscle develop where it had never existed before.

It's no different in our quest to get spiritually fit. It begins with the decision to invest the time and energy, and to start making the effort, little by little. Just talking about how much you need and desire to get serious with God is not going to get you there. You need to take small steps, however daunting they may seem, and then get some good tools: a Bible, journal, books, podcasts, and so forth. Then, as necessary, make adjustments in your schedule to be able to spend time with God, setting your alarm clock a little earlier if necessary and following through.

Getting started is the hardest part. But when you see yourself begin to grow in knowledge of God and His will for your life, and as you begin to experience God speaking to you and guiding your life, the rewards are worth it.

The days of complaining about how unhappy I was with my weight and my inability to wear my favorite clothes had to come to an end. Similarly, when you embark on a training program, the day will come when you see the improvements you long for. Friend, begin somewhere and focus on one day at a time. Stop putting off what you know you need to do and start doing something about it. I know it's not easy, and you may feel a bit daunted at first not knowing where to begin, but help is available if you ask. Before you know it, you will be making great strides and advancing to running on the treadmill, as I was later able to do.

I once heard Joyce Meyer say, "You have to plan your pain to plan your pleasure." I often recall that when I'm running at the gym, for I've learned that getting fit, whether physical or spiritual, is not without some measure of effort or even discomfort at first. However, when you begin to reach those small, incremental goals you've set and see yourself growing in faith and in God's love, you realize it's worth it. Decide to make that commitment and courageously apply God's Word to your life today.

1. What are some other correlations you see between physical and spiritual fitness?

_____

_____

2. Is there an area that seems daunting to you as you think about running with God? Share that with a godly friend and ask for prayer about it.

_____

_____

3. What one area of weakness do you need to especially focus on in your quest for spiritual fitness?

_____

_____

OVERCOMING SPIRITUAL ADD

Until I get there, focus on reading the Scriptures to the church, encouraging the believers, and teaching them. ... Give your complete attention to these matters. Throw yourself into your tasks so that everyone will see your progress.
—1 Timothy 4:13, 15, NLT

Previously we considered how the best way to begin a journey of spiritual growth is by taking small steps. In this section, we will look at a subject that's not only important in the area of sports, but also in this area of spiritual maturity; that is, our need for better *focus*.

If you were to look up the definition of *focus* in a dictionary, you'd find the following:

- to direct toward a particular point or purpose
- a center of activity, attraction, or attention
- a point of concentration[2]

Focus is what directs you toward your ultimate purpose, sharpening your thinking and decisions as you take steps toward becoming spiritually mature. As these definitions imply, focus is what enables you to concentrate on what you are doing and where you are heading. We've seen that runners do not run about aimlessly and boxers do not beat the air carelessly (1 Cor. 9:26). They are intently focused on what they want to accomplish and how they are doing it. We need to learn from them.

Spiritual Attention Deficit Disorder

We live in a world in which choosing to focus on the things of God is almost an old-fashioned concept. Whenever I read history books about the great Christian men and women of the past, I step into passionate periods of history where lives, even nations, were changed by the power of God. People such as George Mueller, William and Catherine Booth, Jonathan Edwards, John Wycliffe, Martin Luther, William Wilberforce, and the like, although they lived in different times and countries, were all focused on and passionate for God and the individual missions He entrusted to them.

Our twenty-first-century world is still in desperate need of men and women who are on fire for God, people who are not afraid to give up their lives to Him and His great causes, people unafraid to take steps of faith and believe Him for the miraculous. We mustn't allow our hearts to be shaped by our media and social culture that teach us to focus on living for our own pleasures and comfort alone.

Our fast-paced, self-gratifying culture is nurturing a generation of people to give their time and attention to things that don't really matter or have lasting value. More than that, because so much in our culture is geared toward doing things easier and faster, we are programmed to expect the same in our spiritual lives. Yet God doesn't operate on a Google basis. So the way things happen in the spiritual realm, such as the need to seek God and sometimes wait for Him or the principle of the harvest, can seem so foreign to us. Growing in God is not like instant noodles we can just add hot water to and enjoy. It's more akin to oven baking: it needs time and the right ingredients and temperature to produce a great result. Dr. Michael Lardon describes the danger of our inattentive culture:

> We live in a culture of attention deficit disorder (ADD). We are bombarded with stimuli at all times, cell phones ringing ... email access at every destination. Our mind's attention is usurped by the seductive interface with modern-day technology. When our attention is pulled in every direction, we paradoxically live in an internal state of chronic

inattentiveness. We may find some bravado in seeing or showing off to others how many things we can do at once—as if multitasking is a sign of higher intelligence. This modern-day cultural phenomenon is toxic and leads to inefficiency and suboptimal performance.[3]

I fear this suboptimal performance has sneaked into our Christian lives. We avoid extending ourselves in ways that could bring any level of discomfort, and it doesn't even occur to us to invest significant time or attention into the things of God.

For many of us, our walk with God is almost accidental, determined by our feelings at the time rather than by deliberate focus and purpose. If we feel like reading the Bible, we will. But if we don't, we won't. If we sense an urgent need, then we'll suddenly find the time to pray, but when things are going well, we say we don't have time. Please understand that such an approach to your spiritual life is not going to reap the fruit you desire. If athletes approached their training programs and daily discipline with the inattentiveness and negligence that many Christians do in their relationships with God, they would quickly find themselves discouraged and defeated.

Whether you are a businessperson, parent, teacher, stockbroker, engineer, or factory worker, you must be focused in order to succeed. Orlick writes, "I have never met an Olympic champion, world champion, or world leader in any field who did not decide that he or she was going to go after his or her goals with full focus. If you want to perform and live to your personal potential, at some point you have to decide to do it with full focus."[4]

Symptoms of Spiritual ADD

It's easy to recognize the symptoms of spiritual sickness and weakness in our lives. Do any of the following sound familiar?

- a lack of confidence in the power of prayer and God Himself
- a lack of knowledge of and confidence in God and His promises
- no real quality time with other believers, resulting in feelings of isolation and loneliness
- overbearing anxiety and worry, and a lack of peace
- an increasingly busy life, resulting in no room for God in your schedule
- compromises with sin
- difficulty in saying no to people
- confusion about God's will
- increasing doubt about God's existence

These are all symptoms of one specific condition: a lack of attention and focus in your walk with God, or spiritual ADD. It doesn't happen overnight, but it's a gradual slippery slope of poor decisions that lead you away from God. Less time in God's Word and prayer, skipped fellowship, compromise with sin—all these lead you away from God, one sneaky step at a time. You've ignored the universal principle that states you get out what you put in, and perhaps you've ignored the need to put boundaries in your life. So how can you begin to change all that? What steps can you take to get back on track and be deliberate in where you are heading spiritually?

Work on Controllable Variables

Sports psychiatrists who coach some of the best athletes in professional sports help their clients realize two things about focus. First, they cannot determine or control some variables in their performance. But they can control others, and those are the ones they need to assume responsibility for. A tennis player, for example, cannot control the weather that might affect the tournament, how well her opponent plays, or an unexpected injury. But she *can* control her personal balance of work and rest, how well she watches her diet, and how well she focuses on each shot during play. Winning athletes focus on those things they can control and affect. Allowing themselves to be distracted by the things they have no control over only leads to frustration.

The same is true for you. There are areas you can focus on improving and others you currently cannot. Some controllable variables may include

- forming a new prayer habit when you're on the way home from a morning school run or on the way to work
- finding a few minutes to read and apply the Bible during quieter moments
- switching off the TV or telephone to eliminate unnecessary distractions in your time with God and to create time to think

- making time for God at a certain time each day
- taking a walk to help you clear your mind and talk to God
- becoming more disciplined in your sleeping habits

As you begin to focus on making small but necessary changes like these, you will immediately reap the benefits. Becoming stronger spiritually begins with small alterations in your schedule and habits. Of course, some commitments you cannot change, but I'm sure you can find some time or make changes somewhere. Understand the importance of disciplined focus in your relationship with God and begin to see where you can make small improvements. As Lardon says, "Generally, the quality of our performance is a function of the intensity of our focus."[5]

As the saying goes, "impossible is nothing."

4. In 1 Timothy 4:13–15, what did Paul advise Timothy to do?

_____

_____

5. What did Paul advise against in verse 14?

_____

_____

6. What one specific area of weakness can you begin to focus on in order to grow spiritually?

_____

_____

YOUR DAYS ARE NUMBERED

Lord, remind me how brief my time on earth will be. Remind me that my days are numbered—how fleeting my life is. You have made my life no longer than the width of my hand.
—Psalm 39:4–5, NLT

Time is one of those things many of us feel we do not have enough of. How many of us have wished for more than twenty-four hours a day? The Bible teaches us that we need to make careful use of our time so we can grow in wisdom and fruitfulness. As Steve Jobs used to say, "Live each day as if it were your last, and someday you'll most certainly be right."

In this section we will look at how we can redeem some of those lost hours from our lives in order to devote them to our spiritual development and overall well-being.

Recoup Lost Time

A wise person is hungry for knowledge,
while the fool feeds on trash.
—Proverbs 15:14, NLT

With all the various forms of distractions and entertainment around us, using our time wisely and finding time for our spiritual strengthening can be quite a challenge. Television, movies, smart phones, computer games, and surfing the Internet are some of the things that compete with investing in our personal growth. Many people, after a hard day's work, like to sit in front of a screen of some sort and spend hours mentally switching off. All over the world, for both the rich and the poor, the TV screen is one of the primary means of relaxation and mental refreshment. Yet we know that everything we watch is not good and profitable. Let's be honest, most of us tend to spend too much time in front of it.

When we spend hours in front of the TV we are essentially allowing ourselves to be discipled and educated by the media. Of course, if you're watching beneficial programs and movies, that's great. Yet we know that's not always the case. In my home I've had to set limits on what kind of programs and movies we watch and allow our family to be influenced by. We do not watch movies or other programs that have a rating we feel uncomfortable with or anything of an occult, very violent, or sexual nature. After all, you cannot "unsee" something once you've watched it. Once you've allowed something into your thinking, it's there for good. Not only do ungodly programs do nothing to help us grow spiritually, they have a detrimental effect on the morality of our families as we allow them to train and shape our thinking, values, and ambitions.

The Lamp of the Body

The eye is the lamp of the body. If your eyes are good, your whole body will be full of light. But if your eyes are bad, your whole body will be full of darkness. If then the light within you is darkness, how great is that darkness!
—Matthew 6:22–23

We may think what we watch doesn't affect our maturity in Christ, but it does. After all, the eye is the lamp of the body, as Jesus explained in this verse. A pastor I knew in the U.K. visited a shopping mall with one of the guys from his church who had brought along his two young children. While sitting down for coffee together to talk, an older couple near them remarked (very seriously) about what a modern family they were and commended their confidence in being seen together as a gay couple in public. When the pastor informed them that he was a pastor having a counseling session with one of his members, they were embarrassed. When I heard this, I was grieved at the influence of the media upon our thinking.

We can allow either the media or God's Word to disciple us, for what we see and hear affects our whole being, good and bad. Spending excessive hours in front of a TV or computer screen every day is not only a poor use of your time, but it also eats into some of the time you should be spending with God. I'm not telling you to throw away your beautiful flat-screen TV, but if you find it hard to find time to devote to your relationship with God, then I encourage you to begin cutting back and redeeming some of those lost hours. Stop watching unprofitable and spiritually detrimental programs and instead find other means of relaxation. Becoming more accountable with your time will not only help you find the time to grow spiritually, it will benefit you overall as a child of God. Let's look at some great examples of how you can do just that.

- *Read and listen.* This may sound old-fashioned, but one terrific way of spending your spare time wisely is by reading or listening to good books (including e-books, audio books, or podcasts). I didn't start reading books seriously as a hobby until my early thirties, but since then I've become a bit obsessed. I have learned so much through reading (mostly Christian) books, and I particularly love reading biographies of great men and women, past and present. Their lives and experiences with God teach us so much about living faithfully. Learning and growing in the knowledge of God as well as in skills and abilities is a far more productive use of our time than watching TV for hours on end. Reading books or listening to podcasts is a fantastic way to unwind and, at the same time, be inspired to grow.
- *Sign up for a course.* Loads of courses, whether online or at your local church or college, are available. These days you can learn anything from cookery and woodwork to evangelism and church history. Whatever field you want to learn and grow in is out there somewhere. After completing my fitness management course last year, I signed up for a basic dressmaking course this year, all because I

simply desired to do something profitable with my Sunday evenings. You get a sense of accomplishment when you've achieved or created something of positive value, and it's a far better use of your time than simply watching TV or surfing the Internet and having nothing to show for your time. It does take effort to do some research and register, but as I'm sure you'll find, it'll be worth it and you'll be glad you did.

- *Join a group.* Another way of using your time wisely is by joining a group of some kind: a small group, Bible study, prayer cell, book club, coffee morning—the list could go on. Ask yourself what area of your life could use some encouragement and growth. Figure it out and then find a group that will meet that need. If you can't find a group, why not start one?
- *Create time for God.* This is one area in which many Christians profess to have difficulty. Whenever I speak to people about carving out time each day for God, they often say they're just too busy. Brothers and sisters, if we find ourselves too busy to spend time with God, then something is not right in our lives, and we clearly need to make some decisions that will redeem some of that time.

Nothing—no responsibility or obligation—should distract you from spending quality time with God. Your time with God provides your much-needed daily nourishment and will enable you to live life firing on all cylinders. It will strengthen you and keep you sane as life whirls around you. You can grow in God only if you spend time with Him. It's that simple. Eric Liddell once said,

> We communicate with God through prayer and Bible study. The best way is to decide upon a definite time for your prayer time, preferably in the early morning, and keep it sacred. Build the habits of your life around that period. Do you allow it to be crowded out by other things? Those who, neglecting the fixed time for prayer, say they can pray at all times, will probably end in praying at no time. But if you keep the fixed period, it should influence the whole day.[6]

Is it really too hard to redeem some of those lost hours in your schedule to assist you in becoming stronger spiritually? Sure, it takes discipline, but it is possible. It all comes down to whether you are willing: "For God has not given us a spirit of fear and timidity, but of power, love, and self-discipline" (2 Timothy 1:7, NLT). According to this verse, you already have the discipline of Christ within you and you can access it *if you are willing.*

It's your responsibility alone to decide how you spend your time: "Teach us to make the most of our time, so that we may grow in wisdom" (Psalm 90:12, NLT).

You have a limited amount of time here on this earth, so use it wisely. Be responsible and find ways to strengthen yourself spiritually and glorify God with your time.

7. Take a few minutes and calculate how many hours per week, on average, you watch TV.

_____

_____

8. How beneficial has your time watching TV, playing computer games, and surfing the Internet been to your life and relationship with God?

_____

_____

9. What is one change you can make to create time with God?

_____

_____

ENERGY SOURCES

I pray that out of his glorious riches he may strengthen you with power through his Spirit in your inner being.
—Ephesians 3:16

As I started trying to get fit physically, I was surprised how much my energy level affected my overall physical performance. I've discovered that whenever my body feels more rested and fed, I'm able to do considerably better during my workouts and in my other daily responsibilities.

In this section, we will look at how our level of energy affects our *spiritual* condition. Toward that end, let's consider several ways we gain energy spiritually and physically, enabling us to better function as an athlete of God.

The Power of Rest

For almost a year, I was going to the gym nearly every day. Then I realized that schedule was having a detrimental effect on my physical strength. Although I was determined to do as much as I could, I eventually found that becoming exhausted made me feel weak at the gym, less motivated, and, as a result, shortened my exercise routines and impacted other areas of my life.

The same holds true for us as we serve God. As a disciple of Christ, we can easily do too much and find it begins to have a detrimental effect on us. Of course, I'm talking about the dangers of burnout. I think of a missionary friend who is on the verge of entering into burnout. She's working so hard in her ministry, serving others, shooting around the city, trying her best to serve God, that she is neglecting her own emotional and physical needs. She doesn't rest or eat enough. As a result, she is beginning to feel drained, depressed, discouraged, and, quite simply, tired. If she continues like this, she will probably reach the point where she is no longer able to do her ministry at all, which of course is not God's plan for her.

The interesting thing about people who do too much and don't rest enough is that they usually know they're doing it. My husband has a tendency to overwork because he loves his job, but he'll be the first to agree he's doing too much and needs to rest more.

When I finally realized I was overdoing my exercise routine, I made the decision to stop pushing myself so hard and cut down the number of days and hours. I also decided to become better disciplined in terms of how much I slept each night. I'm not always successful, but when I am, I can feel the difference physically. I can run longer with less strenuous effort and it becomes a more enjoyable experience. Essentially, because I'm allowing my body enough rest and recovery, because I'm creating a better balance, I'm feeling the benefits. Jim Loehr and Tony Schwartz confirm this:

> Several decades of sports science research have established that the key to increasing physical strength is a phenomenon known as supercompensation— essentially the creation of balanced work-rest ratios. In weightlifting, this involves stressing a muscle to the point where its fibers literally start to break down. Given an adequate period of recovery (typically at least 48 hours), the muscle will not only heal, it will grow stronger. But persist in stressing the muscle without rest and the result will be acute and chronic damage. Conversely, the failure to stress the muscle results in weakness and atrophy.[7]

Whatever your daily demands and responsibilities may be, whether you're working full time outside the home or inside the home, you need to rest your body and allow it to recover. You may be wondering why I'm talking so much about physical rest and balance. I'm sure you'd agree that our physical condition greatly affects how we feel and respond spiritually. I have a number of wonderful Christian friends who readily admit they burn the midnight oil too much and are not able to spend quality time the next day with God simply because they feel too tired.

When you give yourself enough rest, you find you have more energy and strength to not only better fulfill your daily responsibilities, but also to spend the quality time with God you know you need. Don't give in to the temptation to push yourself too hard and burn out. God is able to provide help and assistance where you need it, if you ask Him. Your physical condition impacts you spiritually and emotionally, so start taking better care of yourself.

Spiritual Nutrition

Of course, what we eat is an essential source of energy. All the books and experts say you need enough of the right foods, especially protein, to repair and strengthen your broken muscle tissue. You are what you eat, whether that's physical or spiritual. If you want to be strong spiritually, you have to nourish yourself on the right kind of spiritual food. As Christians, our main source of spiritual food is the Word of God: "It is written: Man does not live on bread alone, but on every word that comes from the mouth of God" (Matthew 4:4).

Our strength and vigor come from God and His Word. It was true even for Jesus, who spoke these words. His point was that God and His Word alone provide us with the spiritual protein, vitamins, and carbohydrates we need in life. I don't have to tell you that neglecting God's Word causes you to feel weaker. Anyone who has been a follower of Christ for some time already understands that.

Those who choose to not feed themselves on the food of God's Word feel the lack spiritually: they feel further from God, they struggle to hear His voice, they are weakened in their prayer life, and they start compromising with sin. It's like a vicious circle: the less you eat of God's Word, the weaker you feel and the less motivated you are. That's why proper nutrition is so important. I love how Eric Liddell described the experience of taking proper time to feed oneself with God's Word: "Don't read hurriedly. Every word is precious. Pause, assimilate. When a person hurries through a wood, few birds and animals appear. They hide. But if he sits down and waits, they come out. It will be so with reading the Bible and praying. ... Expose your inmost being to his Word. Be willing to obey, and *obey*."[8]

We will look at this subject in more depth in the following chapter.

Mutual Encouragement

Another powerful energy source for us spiritually is receiving encouragement from other believers. Encouragement is a powerful source of strength, while discouragement can be defeating and debilitating. We all need a little encouragement sometimes in our walks with God. Some great sources include

- meeting in Christian fellowship through a small group or Bible study
- finding one or two prayer partners to share and pray with regularly
- reading testimonies or books about the working of God
- listening to sermons

Even the early disciples of Christ understood the need and power of mutual encouragement in the faith, as the following verses show:

> We sent Timothy, who is our brother and God's fellow worker in spreading the gospel of Christ, to strengthen and encourage you in your faith, so that no one would be unsettled by these trials. You know quite well we were destined for them (1 Thessalonians 3:2–3).

> The men were sent off and went down to Antioch, where they gathered the church together and delivered the letter. The people read it and were glad for its encouraging message. Judas and Silas, who themselves were prophets, said much to encourage and strengthen the brothers (Acts 15:30–32).

These Scriptures show how the believers were encouraged by one another, and how that encouragement had the power to significantly strengthen them in their faith. When was the last time you had some real fellowship with another Christian friend? Have you enjoyed the blessing of someone praying for you or with you recently? You need to be strengthened and encouraged in your daily walk with God, and so I urge you to find opportunities where that can happen. Go and find some good fellowship. Your faith needs it.

God has provided some wonderful sources of energy that we need in order to thrive as followers of Christ. Understand the importance of each of these areas we've looked at and, as you do, you will find yourself growing stronger and stronger.

10. Think of a time when you received encouragement from someone. How did that make you feel?

_____

_____

11. Have you encouraged someone recently? How did you do that?

_____

_____

12. Are you getting enough rest? If not, what practical changes can you make to be sure that happens?

_____

_____

WALK IN GOD'S MIRACULOUS POWER

*I pray also that the eyes of your heart may be enlightened
in order that you may know the hope to which he has called
you, the riches of his glorious inheritance in the saints,
and his incomparably great power for us who believe.*
—Ephesians 1:18–19

If you are a follower of Jesus Christ, you have God's great power dwelling in you. That's what the Bible says. Think about that statement for a moment.

Most if not all Christians believe God is all-powerful and can do anything He wills. However, when we think of God's power and miracles, we usually think only of the great miracles of the past that we read about in the Bible. But we don't understand that God wants to move in power among us *today*. Or if we do, we think He only does such work among believers who live in the poorest or toughest parts of the globe, as they have nothing or no one else to depend on.

Why do we have such low expectations of God moving in power in our lives? Where did that thinking come from? Like Gideon, we lament how God's great miracles are no longer seen today and assume God has left us (Judges 6:13). We look back in awe and reverence at God's great miracles of the past and wrongly conclude that God no longer works like that.

Such a viewpoint is unbiblical. Has God changed? Have the needs of mankind changed or God's promises been altered? Do people no longer need to see God's power and glory displayed? Of course not! We still need to see God's power and love displayed in our lives.

I'm sure you know people, believers and not-yet believers, who have a desperate need to see God move in answer to their prayers—to see loved ones saved, sickness healed, infertility overcome, financial needs met, painful memories healed, jobs acquired, and so on. Many of us would love to see the power of God move in our own lives and in the lives of our loved ones. The good news is, my friend, God is a wonderful and kind God who loves to meet our every need: "I will tell of the kindnesses of the Lord, the deeds for which he is to be praised, according to all the Lord has done for us—yes, the many good things he has done ... according to his compassion and many kindnesses" (Isaiah 63:7).

Let me make the point again: God is kinder and more compassionate than you know. His generosity and love have not changed; neither has man's need, nor His Word and promises. It is only our perspective and understanding that have sadly, wrongly changed. To personally experience the power of God today in ways we read about in Scripture, we need to grasp several Biblical principles.

Live by Faith

As you look at the miracles of both the Old and New Testaments, you will find one common theme: the people of God experienced God's power after they had taken an act or step of faith. For example:

- The Red Sea divided after Moses raised his staff over the water (Exodus 14).
- The Jordan River was divided after the priests put their feet into the water (Joshua 3).
- Goliath was slain after David ran toward him and threw a stone (1 Samuel 17).
- Jonathan saw victory over twenty Philistines after he climbed a cliff with his hands and feet (1 Samuel 14).
- Naaman was healed of leprosy after he dipped himself in the Jordan seven times (2 Kings 5).
- Simon Peter caught the biggest catch of fish in his life after he let down the nets at Jesus' seemingly illogical instruction (Luke 5).
- Simon Peter received money for the temple tax from the mouth of a fish after throwing out a fishing line as Jesus instructed (Matthew 17:27).
- The woman subject to bleeding for twelve years was healed after she reached out and touched Jesus' clothing (Mark 5).

- Zechariah, father of John the Baptist, was healed of his muteness after he wrote John's name on a tablet (Luke 1:63).
- The blind beggar received his sight after desperately calling for Jesus' attention (Luke 18:35–43).
- Paul and Silas were miraculously released from prison after a prayer and worship session (Acts 16).

All of these people have two things in common: first, they received a wonderful miracle from God's hand, and second, they exercised their faith first to receive it.

When we make a move of faith, it does something in us and in the spiritual realm. When you put yourself out there and take a physical step of faith of some kind, you are saying to God, "I really do believe in you," and it releases His power in the spiritual realm as a result. It's a real and powerful spiritual principle:

Faith first, then the miracle.

When you take a stand of faith and declare, "I really believe what God's Word says and will behave accordingly," God responds and you experience His faithfulness to His Word. That is why so many people around the world who are hungry and desperate enough to reach out to God and really believe and live by His Word are experiencing His power and miracles. They are not afraid of looking foolish. They know God is the only One who can help them, and they believe accordingly. They place their faith in God because their lives often literally depend on it. Countless people all over the world today are experiencing physical healings, deliverances, practical and financial provisions, and even raisings from the dead because they simply believe God and His Word and live like they do. They are experiencing what it means to live in the power of God's Holy Spirit. God can do the same for you. You just need to act in faith.

Live by God's Word

Living by God's Word is powerful for it's there we find answers to our every need:

- financial needs met no matter how impossible it seems
- a job despite the difficult economy
- healing for the whole person: physical, mental, emotional, and spiritual
- answers to prayer about childlessness
- provision of a marriage partner as you learn to love God first and foremost
- guidance from God as you acknowledge and trust in Him with all your heart
- comfort to the brokenhearted as you draw near to Him

There is no need God cannot meet. Invest the time into reading the Bible to discover the precious promises of God. A sincere study of Scripture will lead you to no other conclusion than a confidence in God and His faithfulness. Our God is a good and compassionate God who wants to reveal and glorify Himself among us. After all, that is what answers to prayer actually do—they reveal God to us and those around us. I often tell my not-yet-believing family members what I'm praying about so that when God answers, they will know He has done a miracle, which will bring them one step nearer to God.

Dear brothers and sisters, knowing and living by God's Word will empower and strengthen you enormously:

> For the eyes of the Lord range throughout the earth to strengthen those whose hearts are fully committed to him (2 Chronicles 16:9).

> I can do everything through him who gives me strength (Philippians 4:13).

Know and understand the power and resources of God available to you. Don't listen to the lies of the enemy who will try to convince you God doesn't move in such ways today and that you cannot accomplish anything great for God's kingdom. The Bible teaches us that we are the dwelling place of God by His Holy Spirit (1 Corinthians 3:16). Dare to believe the Word of God. Ponder on the following words of the great nineteenth-century missionary to China, Hudson Taylor:

> Many Christians estimate difficulty in the light of their own resources, and thus they attempt very little and they always fail. All giants have been weak men who did great things for God because they reckoned on His power and presence to be with them.

Since the days of Pentecost, has the whole church ever put aside every other work and waited upon Him for ten days, that the Spirit's power might be manifested? We give too much attention to method and machinery and resources, and too little to the source of power.[9]

Either we believe God and the promises of His Word and live like we do, or we don't. To draw on God's power will require that you step out in faith and believe God's Word. As you do, you too will experience God's incomparably great power in your life that Paul the apostle wrote about in our opening verses of Ephesians 1. Start drawing on His power and learn how to walk by faith.

13. Read 1 Corinthians 4:20. According to this verse, what is the kingdom of God about?

_____

_____

14. Now read 2 Corinthians 4:7–10 and 2 Corinthians 12:8–10. What do our weaknesses give us the opportunity to experience?

_____

_____

15. Read Ephesians 3:16 and 20. What does verse 16 promise us? What does verse 20 reveal about what God wants to do for us?

_____

_____

APPLICATION QUESTIONS

Prayerfully answer the following questions. Ask the Lord to guide you and speak to your heart.

1. Read 1 Corinthians 9:27. What did Paul do to develop himself?

   _____

   _____

2. What is one area in which you need to improve your focus? Can you think of some ways you can do that?

   _____

   _____

3. What is one energy source you have found helpful in the past?

   _____

   _____

4. Is there an area of your life in which you need to see the power of God move? Find appropriate promises of God that will feed your faith, and pray accordingly.

    _____

    _____

5. Read Hebrews 12:11. In what ways have you experienced God's discipline and how did it help you grow?

    _____

    _____

6. Now read Ecclesiastes 7:2. What was the intention of the writer in these words? How can you apply them?

    _____

    _____

7. What is one area God has spoken to you about through this chapter? How will you respond to Him?

    _____

    _____

Chapter 5
NUTRITION

Do you not know that your body is a temple of the Holy Spirit, who is in you, whom you have received from God? You are not your own; you were bought at a price. Therefore honor God with your body.
—1 Corinthians 6:19–20

I have a love-hate relationship with food. I love the taste of food, I love the feeling of being comfortably full, and I love enjoying a meal together with family and friends.

The same food that provides me with nourishment and energy became for me a big source of comfort. I remember sneaking cookies, eating an extra piece of cake, and indulging on elaborate meals that were much too large for me. Food became not only a comfort blanket for me, but also a reward and even a friend. Whether I felt high or low, I looked to food for my satisfaction. I was more than an emotional eater; I was a marathon eater.

This problem with overconsumption caused me to have problems with my weight and also my skin. I truly believe *greasy foods cause acne. How can we feed our bodies junk food and expect to have beautiful results?* My physical appearance became a source of shame for me, which caused me to have low self-esteem, a withdrawn personality, and a non-existent dating life. I was living like a slave to my self-indulgent behaviors; I felt out of control and unable to make a change.

After eating my way through puberty, my mind cleared and I was left with an unhealthy body image and no real sense of identity. I had tried to validate myself through food, but when that didn't work I turned to getting male attention and then traveling. None of these endeavors led to any real sense of security or satisfaction. This is not to say these sources of enjoyment are wrong, but I discovered after a lot of heartache that they are only meant to be enjoyed in the proper context, which God laid out in the Bible.

I remember feeling hopeless, worthless, ashamed, and disillusioned. Having grown up in church, I knew God was there and I understood He loved me on some levels, but I still had a spiritual disconnect. I had been living to satisfy the desires of the flesh, but the Bible clearly tells us to "live by the Spirit and you will not gratify the desires of the sinful nature. For the sinful nature desires what is contrary to the Spirit, and the Spirit what is contrary to the sinful nature. They are in conflict with each other, so that you do not do what you want" (Galatians 5:16–17). I wanted to be healthy and beautiful, but my actions were counterproductive to achieving my goal.

It took a decision of my will to surrender to God and ask the Holy Spirit to help me step-by-step. It is still a daily commitment to surrender my will and look to God as the source of my validation. I am thankful God has freed me from the *addiction to food, male attention, and an unhealthy view of traveling. Through His Word, my spiritual food, God spoke to me and changed my perspectives forever: "'Everything is permissible for me'—but not everything is beneficial. 'Everything is permissible for me'—but I will not be mastered by anything" (1 Corinthians 6:12).*

God fed my soul and brought the freedom and change I needed. Since then, God has led me on a journey to obtain qualifications in the fields of nutrition and education, and He has also been healing my deepest wounds. God's ways for our lives are indeed perfect and good.

Mary

STEP UP AND FEED YOURSELF

*Do not let this Book of the Law depart from your
mouth; meditate on it day and night, so that you
may be careful to do everything written in it.
Then you will be prosperous and successful.*
—Joshua 1:8

Adventurer Bear Grylls believes that good health is the result
of about 80 percent diet and 20 percent fitness. It's not just
about how we exert ourselves physically, but it's also about
how good a job we're doing feeding ourselves.

Speak to any group of athletes and they'll quickly tell
you the importance of a healthy diet and lifestyle and the
role they play in their overall performance and energy levels.
Because of the increased calories they burn, sportspeople
use far more nutrients and minerals than the average person
and therefore need to ensure they're fully replenishing what
their bodies spend. A lack of proper and sufficient nutrition
can, over time, lead to physical weaknesses and problems
and, if neglected, can even lead to degenerative diseases.

Just as we need proper physical nutrition, we also need
a healthy supply of spiritual vitamins and nutrition—the
next important aspect in our training model. Earlier in the
book we looked at the importance of applying God's Word
in order to live by the Spirit, and also the importance of taking the necessary time to feed ourselves on God's Word. In
this chapter, we will look at the necessary components of a
healthy spiritual diet in more depth and begin to formulate
a personal training program toward spiritual growth.

A Malnourished Diet

As the saying goes, you are what you eat. We all know how a poor diet with insufficient protein and nutrients, and an oversupply of sugar and carbohydrates, can have a detrimental effect upon our health and physical well-being. As personal trainer Gabriel Sey, puts it: "Diet is the most important part of my training. Get it wrong and it's detrimental. ... Make sure you get your diet right. It all starts in the kitchen, not the gym."[1]

Fitness begins in the kitchen.

The same is true in our relationship with God. Our spiritual fitness begins in the "kitchen," the place where we prepare our spiritual nourishment. How we feed our heart and mind has a direct influence upon our spiritual condition, as the following Scripture clearly portrays:

> Though by this time you ought to be teachers, you need someone to teach you the elementary truths of God's word all over again. You need milk, not solid food! Anyone who lives on milk, being still an infant, is not acquainted with the teaching about righteousness. But solid food is for the mature, who by constant use *have trained themselves* to distinguish good from evil (Hebrews 5:12–14, emphasis added).

The writer of these verses understood the relationship between what we eat spiritually and our level of progress and maturity. Imagine seeing a grown man walking around wearing a diaper, having a bottle of milk for lunch. Yet there are many who fail to progress out of the diaper stage as Christians, who walk around bypassing the meat, fruit, and vegetables and who are happy to content themselves on milk alone. The result is a generation of spiritual babes, crying out for someone to feed them, not using their own two arms and legs to do it themselves.

If you're a parent, I'm sure you can appreciate how insufficient nutrition impedes growth for the young. Yet how responsible are we for our own spiritual growth? Friend, you can't depend on others to feed and enable your spiritual growth. You must begin to learn to stand on your own two feet.

Symptoms of Malnourishment

Your "kitchen," the place where you feed yourself, is vital. Your personal growth and maturity significantly depends on how well you feed and train yourself in the disciplines of God's Word, prayer, and worship. Neglecting to nourish yourself on the spiritual food of the Bible and prayer leads to spiritual malnourishment. You may look well-fed on the outside, but the truth is, you are spiritually emaciated on the inside.

Check your level of nourishment by asking yourself the following questions:

- Do I have an understanding of God's will for my life?
- Am I setting aside a time each day to pray?
- Do I feel beset by worry or fear about my life?
- Am I able to sleep peacefully at night?

- Am I walking with the peace of God in my heart?
- Do I believe the promises and application of God's Word for my life?
- Do I love God?
- Am I seriously considering compromise in something I know is not God's will?
- Do I find myself losing interest in the things of God and His church?
- Do I have a desire to do God's will in my life?
- Am I serving Him?
- Am I responding to relationship difficulties with God's grace, or do I find myself acting like everyone else in the world around me?

How you answer these questions will clearly reveal whether you are taking in enough spiritual food and nutrition. Make every effort to eat sufficient calories spiritually, nourishing yourself with things of God that will benefit you. You are what you eat: "He humbled you, causing you to hunger and then feeding you with manna, which neither you nor your fathers had known, to teach you that man does not live on bread alone but on every word that comes from the mouth of the Lord" (Deuteronomy 8:3).

1. According to Deuteronomy 8:3, what did God want the Israelites to understand?

   _____

   _____

2. Can you think of a situation that God used to humble you in order to encourage you to depend more on Him?

_____

_____

3. On a scale of 1–10, how healthy is your current spiritual diet?

_____

_____

WHOLESOME DIET

Brothers, I could not address you as spiritual but as worldly—mere infants in Christ. I gave you milk, not solid food, for you were not yet ready for it. Indeed, you are still not ready. You are still worldly. For since there is jealously and quarrelling among you, are you not worldly? Are you not acting like mere men?
—1 Corinthians 3:1–3

Previously we looked at the importance of feeding ourselves with a proper, nutritious spiritual diet. We also observed some of the symptoms that result when we fail to do so. Next we will examine what a good and sufficient diet looks like.

A Good Diet Is Regular

Sporadic visits to the gym don't pay off much in terms of physical fitness. The same is true for us spiritually. Reading the Bible and praying on an irregular basis isn't going to benefit you anywhere near as much as if you engage in these disciplines regularly and consistently. We have great ambitions of losing weight when a new year comes round and the regret of overeating at Christmas sets in. In the same way, we can have great intentions of growing in our relationships with God when we feel a particular need, but we will grow only as we *regularly* invest our time and effort. How serious and committed we are to getting fit spiritually will be seen in how often we bring ourselves into God's presence. Consider Daniel's example: "When Daniel learned that the decree had been published, he went home to his upstairs room where the windows opened toward Jerusalem. Three times a day he got down on his knees and prayed, giving thanks to his God, just as he had done before" (Daniel 6:10).

Daniel lived in dark times spiritually and was surrounded by people who didn't worship the living God. His colleagues openly practiced all kinds of ungodly beliefs: astrology, sorcery, and magic, to name a few (Daniel 2:2–5, 10). So how did he survive in such an ungodly and challenging environment? He disciplined himself and regularly spent time with God in prayer and His Word. Not only did he survive and thrive spiritually, but he stood out from all those around him.

A Good Diet Is Balanced

Some people do well in one area of spiritual discipline but completely overlook others to the detriment of their relationship with God. For example, a friend of mine is a wonderful prayer warrior but she rarely reads the Bible, and I see how she struggles as a result. She doesn't know how to handle difficult relationships in her office; she doesn't understand the goodness of God's character; and she struggles with doubts, fears, and her temper. If only she poured herself into God's Word as much as she prayed, she would fare much better in her daily life. But because she chooses not to, she is weak and vulnerable in many areas. While it is wonderful she is praying regularly and asking God to show her what to do, the answers she desires are often found in God's Word, if only she would pick it up.

A good spiritual diet is balanced, and by that I mean we need to invest in the various spiritual practices, such as Bible study and application, prayer, and worship. You need vitamins and minerals as well as protein and carbohydrates. If you feed yourself in each of these areas, you will become mature and balanced. You will discover God's will for your life, how to handle the storms of life, and how to grow into a spiritually fit believer.

A Good Diet Avoids Junk Food

We know we shouldn't eat junk food, but it tastes so good! I admit I like a nice bar of chocolate now and again. Not truffles or anything fancy, but the good, old-fashioned kind, and especially chocolate mints (particularly when they've been refrigerated). Whenever I return to the U.K. for a visit, the temptation is particularly strong as chocolate seems to be everywhere! I invested a good portion of my time last year to getting fit physically; if I bought and ate chocolate every time I fancied it, I would soon lose all the rewards of my gym investment.

It's not enough to exercise regularly; we also need to avoid junk food, which defeats any progress we make. This requires exercising self-discipline and limiting the amount of "treats" we allow ourselves (unless you're like my good friend Sian who can eat chocolate any time of day or night and not put on weight). As Mary testified in her story at the start of this chapter, too much junk food can stop being just a nice treat and instead turn into something harmful.

What is spiritual junk food for believers? Junk food includes:

- violent or immoral TV programs or movies
- pornographic material
- gossip or slander
- ungodly websites
- spending time with people who pull you away from God

I may be coming across as an old-fashioned, conservative fuddy-duddy, but I believe too many believers today allow the garden of their minds and hearts to be exposed to all kinds of ungodly influence, with no fences or protection to keep the garbage out. It's a fact of life that if we spend our time excessively feeding our hearts and minds with the things of the world, we will inevitably be negatively affected by it. Why? Because we are what we think and all these things have a way of significantly influencing how we think and, therefore, how we live. Remember, all things are permissible, but not all things are beneficial (1 Corinthians 6:12). Anything or anyone that draws you away from God should be considered "junk food." Be wise and avoid anything that will damage or hinder your spiritual growth and progress.

I pray you will give serious thought to the quality and regularity of your spiritual diet, and that you will plan how to create the time you need to invest in it. May God bless and strengthen you as you become more spiritually fit.

4. What are some good habits you are currently doing that are benefiting your spiritual growth?

_____

_____

5. Can you think of any practical ways you can make your diet more balanced and regular?

_____

_____

6. What area of "junk food" is hindering you spiritually and do you need to give up?

_____

_____

DEVELOP YOUR MUSCLE

*For physical training is of some value, but godliness
has value for all things, holding promise for
both the present life and the life to come.*
—1 Timothy 4:8

Every successful athlete has a tailored workout regimen. This
may sound a bit strange, talking about workout regimens
in the area of spiritual development, but I truly believe the
Bible teaches that God will bless our efforts as we train
ourselves. That is, *if* we pray, *if* we read and apply God's
Word, *if* we learn how to take steps of faith, *if* we begin to
use our spiritual gifts, and so on, we will reap the rewards.

Guaranteed Returns

*Do not be deceived: God cannot be mocked. A man reaps
what he sows. The one who sows to please his sinful
nature, from that nature will reap destruction; the one who
sows to please the Spirit, from the Spirit will reap eternal
life. Let us not become weary in doing good, for at the
proper time we will reap a harvest if we do not give up.*
—Galatians 6:7–9

These verses teach us the important principle of investing and return. In other words, we get out what we put in,
a principle that operates in all areas of life.

Athletes understand this well. They know that to improve
a particular ability and strengthen an area of weakness, they
must invest the time and energy into the required training

program. Michael Phelps, Andre Agassi, Rory McIlroy, and Yuna Kim didn't become the great champions they did without sweat, sacrifice, and great effort. Every sportsperson knows that to develop their muscles and skills, and increase their stamina and strength, they must train and develop themselves on a regular basis.

Regular Training

Whatever the sport may be, the degree of growth and improvement correlates directly to the level of training an athlete puts in. Strength training is not without some degree of discomfort.

One day at the gym I spent thirty minutes running on the treadmill and was really proud of my effort. I happened to look to the right and saw a guy a few treadmills away who was running 30 percent faster and had burned 50 percent more calories. He was calm, relaxed, and didn't even appear red in the face. I, on the other hand, had sweat oozing from all my pores. I was amazed at how he was able to run considerably faster, harder, and longer with less apparent strain on his body. Clearly his body was stronger than mine because he had trained it to reach that level of fitness and strength. This same concept carries over into our spiritual growth: we get out what we put in. God doesn't do the training for us.

As 1 Timothy 4 commands, train to be godly. Understand that for your faith to grow, your understanding of God's Word to deepen, your prayer life to develop, and your love for others to blossom, you must invest. That is, you need to spend time with God daily in the things that will benefit you spiritually. As you fulfill your responsibility, God will do His part. Create the best "training program" (more on that later in this chapter) that suits you and stick to it on a regular basis. Frequency and consistency are crucial. If you neglect to invest and flex your spiritual muscles on a regular basis, you will experience atrophy, just as any athlete does. Kimberly Nunley writes,

> Most muscle atrophy is a result of a lack of physical activity. According to the University of Maryland Medical Center, atrophy is typically because people do not use their muscles enough. Those who have physical limitations, become injured or choose to be sedentary will see a shrinking of their muscle tissue. Those who are very physically active and participate in muscle-building activity of strength training will notice their muscles shrinking once they stop lifting weights or decrease their training volume."[2]

If we fail to exercise and discipline ourselves spiritually on a regular basis, we too are in danger of wasting away. For the remainder of this chapter, we are going to look at creating a personal and tailored training program.

Prepare a Comprehensive Training Program

Most athletes who strength train at the gym focus on developing various areas of their body: core muscles, legs, arms, and also the heart and lungs (cardio). Imagine how someone would look if he focused only on his leg muscles or arms. He would look rather unbalanced. Similarly, we need a comprehensive workout when it comes to spiritual strength training.

Core Muscles

Our core muscles (back, hips and abdominals) support our stability and balance and also prevent injury. As Christians we too have core muscles when it comes to spiritual strength training. The following two practices are absolutely essential to our spiritual growth, habits we simply cannot survive without.

Invest in God's Word. As we have already seen, this is by far the most important component in your training program. You simply cannot grow spiritually, know God's will, and live by the Spirit if you do not learn and apply the Bible. The good news is, these days many more tools exist to bring yourself under God's Word: online Bibles or Bible apps on your phone or computer, audio Bibles you can listen to while you're on the go, as well as Bibles or devotional books you can read while commuting. So even if your schedule is super busy, you have enormous choices when it comes to reading and learning what the Bible teaches on how to know God and His will for your life. You really have no excuse!

Find time to pray privately. How can you develop a relationship with God if you are not sharing your heart with Him and not listening to what He has to say? Of course, we are encouraged to pray continually, even on the go, and that's wonderful. But that doesn't replace finding a private time and place to pray. As Jesus taught us in Matthew 6:6, and as He practiced Himself (Luke 5:16), we need to find a place away from distractions where we can pray to our heavenly Father.

Prayer is essential to developing your relationship with God—entering His presence and bringing your concerns to Him. In that special place, God will mold and shape your heart according to His will and speak to you by His Spirit. As you come before God in prayer, you will encounter Him as He ministers to your heart and soul.

Arms

Our arm muscles, spiritually speaking, are God's commands to us to extend ourselves by serving Him by serving others. I can think of at least two ways you can reach out to help and build up your brothers and sisters in Christ.

Use your spiritual gifts. The Bible teaches that we all have spiritual gifts entrusted to us to strengthen and encourage one another. Discover your spiritual gifts and find ways you can develop and use them to serve others.[3] Don't hide behind shyness or humility. That's not God's will, for in Scripture God commands us to use and develop our gifts. Once you know what your gifts are, find a way to use them to serve others, whether within or outside the church.

Use your practical resources. You can also reach out to help others by giving of your resources such as time or money. As you take steps of faith and obedience to serve others, in no time you will find yourself being stretched and growing. After all, how can you fulfill God's command to love your neighbors unless you are willing to serve and bless them? Find your place in the body of Christ and reach out and help others.

Legs

Your leg muscles enable you to run faster, not just on the track, but also in your relationship with God. You can do some specific exercises that will enable you to make significant strides in your faith development. There's a big difference between walking with God and running with Him. So how do you do this?

Stretch yourself. The Bible describes faith as being sure of what we hope for and certain of what we do not see (Hebrews 11:1). God desires that we live not according to what we see with our physical eyes alone, but by what we cannot yet see. In other words, we walk through life by *taking steps of faith*. As we do, two things happen: first, we find our faith being stretched; and second, we see God responding to our faith by His power. Both of these experiences ultimately cause our faith to grow. For Simon Peter, taking a step of faith meant stepping out of a boat in the middle of a storm (Matthew 14:29); for Joshua and the Israelites, it was circling the city of Jericho for seven days and not engaging in any of the usual tactics of war to see the walls fall (Joshua 6).

The best way to fast track your faith is by obeying God's promptings. There's nothing like obedience to God to enable you to grow in Him. Perhaps God has been talking to you about a specific area of your life, but you've been putting off responding to Him. Don't delay. You gain absolutely nothing from delayed obedience, which is essentially disobedience.

Another terrific way you can allow yourself to be stretched is by going on a mission trip or joining a small group where you will be encouraged and challenged in your relationship with God. As you obey God and allow your faith to be stretched, God's power is unleashed from the heavenly realms, and your pace with God will never again be the same.

Everyone's walk with God is unique, but what I've just shared are some practical and important ways you can grow and develop your various muscles groups, spiritually speaking. If, however, you neglect one particular area, you will encounter difficulties or weaknesses in your faith. If you feel you are weak in a specific area, consider whether it's due to neglect of one of the aforementioned muscle groups. To become a balanced and mature disciple of Christ, you need to invest and strengthen yourself in every one of the above areas. As you begin to create your own regular training program and put it into practice, you will feel the difference immediately. Allow yourself to be stretched and challenged because that's when the real growth and blessing happens.

Training Equipment

A final important aspect of strength training is having the right kind of tools. Just as any gym has many different kinds of equipment to stimulate various muscles, many resources are available to help you grow spiritually. These include:

- worship music
- smartphone apps
- online sermons and Bible studies
- podcasts
- books on Christian topics

- mentors and teachers
- small groups

These tools will assist you immensely in your quest to become stronger. Remember, none of them is an end in itself but merely a means to an end: developing the walk with God you've always wanted. Take time to visit your local Christian bookstore or visit one online. Get involved in your local church and join a small group or Bible study. Check out my free iPhone app, *10 Steps to Knowing God,* which has lots of helpful devotions and memorization tools. Make the most of the tools and resources God has put around you to create a great spiritual training program for yourself.

Don't just depend on church services or your leaders to feed you once a week. I don't know any athlete who can win a race by exercising just once or twice a week. I know if I work out like that, my muscles will quickly weaken and I will soon put the pounds back on. Determine to invest in each of these areas and you will soon develop spiritual muscle and reap the benefits. "What benefit did you reap at that time from the things you are now ashamed of? Those things result in death! But now that you have been set free from sin and have become slaves to God, the benefit you reap leads to holiness, and the result is eternal life" (Romans 6:21–22).

7. What is the best time of the day or night for you to read (or listen to) your Bible?

_____

_____

8. What is one quiet place you can pray without distractions from others?

_____

_____

9. What is something God has entrusted to you which you can use to bless others (for instance, time, money, gifts)?

_____

_____

SMALL STEPS, BIG GOALS

So we make it our goal to please him, whether
we are at home in the body or away from it.
—2 Corinthians 5:9

Developing a training program to grow stronger in your relationship with God may sound bizarre, but why not give it a try? After all, without clear spiritual goals and direction, how can you progress? Even Jesus had goals during His time here on earth. When the Pharisees told Jesus that Herod wanted to kill Him, Jesus replied, "Go and tell that fox, 'I will drive out demons and heal people today and tomorrow, and on the third day I will reach my goal'" (Luke 13:32).

Importance of Goals

Becoming a mature disciple of Christ is not something we should leave completely to God. Of course, God has a plan for our lives and we must seek after that. Yet we too have a responsibility and a big part to play toward fulfilling that. We do not fall into becoming the person God desires us to be; as with anything in life, we need to put the time and effort into growing in our faith and His purpose for our lives. Olympic gold medalist Beckie Scott shares the key to personal development and success in her sport:

> I think initially it was the very thorough and detailed process of planning, executing, and evaluating that lay the groundwork for me and became the base for getting the best out of myself mentally in training, racing, and, ultimately, life. It was a step-by-step, day-by-day process that was in motion year-round. The process was always dedicated to improvement, the highest quality, and getting to where I wanted to go. ... I asked myself almost every day, *What am I going to do today to get closer to my goals? How am I going to do it?* And at the end of the day I asked myself, *What went well, and what could I have done better?* ... Developing and implementing a detailed race plan was another one of the crucial elements of my success.[4]

For Beckie to grow and become successful required the creation of a detailed plan of day-by-day goals she needed to accomplish toward her ultimate ambition and purpose.

It required effort, time, and commitment on her part. She needed to be single-minded in her focus, which eventually enabled her to see her dream realized and become an Olympic champion.

Becoming mature in your faith doesn't happen overnight but is the result of faithfully sticking to a daily plan. Chris Zaremba, the founder and CEO of Fitness Over Fifty, talks about obtaining better physical health and nutrition:

> As is so often the case, small steps lead to major achievements—that is as long as you keep taking the small steps. My willpower coped better with making small changes at intervals rather than attempting major change. The transition from my old way of eating to the new way took around a year, during which time I gradually dropped the nasty old habits and incorporated new, healthy eating ones. ... I knew where I started from and I knew where I wanted to go, but the process of reaching the end was a gradual process of small steps.[5]

Friend, as you begin to plan your training program, focus on what you can do today. As you do your part, God will bless your efforts and enable you to grow.

Start Somewhere, Start Small

One morning I was at the gym, sweating it out with everyone else there. Toward the end of my workout, I overheard a conversation between two women—one who was tanned and toned and looked like she really didn't need to be there, and her somewhat bigger friend. She was talking to her friend about an eight-week program she and a few others had decided to embark on. The program consisted of running or cycling at least forty-five minutes a day, plus muscle strengthening six days a week. In response, her poor friend kept asking, "Six days a week?" She was obviously feeling overwhelmed. I felt sorry for this woman, who was clearly already struggling with the treadmill and floor exercises and was nowhere near as fit as her tanned and toned friend. I'm sure her friend meant well, but I cannot help but think that this woman—who I'm sure was, until then, feeling very pleased with herself that day—now felt defeated and discouraged.

We all have to start somewhere. Accomplishing our goals begins by taking realistic, small steps. It's of no benefit whatsoever to compare yourself with someone else on their journey. Instead, start with some realistic goals for yourself and just take small steps toward them.

As Megan shared in her story at the start of Chapter 4, it is the sum of the small things we do faithfully that enable us reach our ultimate, long-term goals. We may think the "short runs"—the small things we do to draw closer to God day by day—don't matter, but they do. Top sports psychologist James E. Loehr explains the principles of goal making to the sports clients he coaches:

- Always give first priority to targeting your training goals toward overcoming weakness.
- Put your plan down in black and white and put it where you will see it every day.

- Set goals that expose you to stress (pushing you, but not leading to overtraining).
- Center your strategic plan around *performance goals* rather than *outcome goals.*[6]

Loehr believes that if we invest our energy into performance goals—those things we *can* control—the rest will happen automatically. It's true: when we get stuck on the "where we should be" (outcome), we lose focus on the day-to-day goals and journey to getting there. Loehr goes on to explain that "it all begins with a dream for the future, and it all happens with what you do today."[7]

My friend Megan quickly appreciated how her smaller runs during the week not only prepared her to accomplish the bigger goal of finishing a marathon, but they also gave her a sense of accomplishment along the way. This in turn created greater confidence and motivation, which she needed.

Examples of overambitious goals include promising yourself you will read the Bible in one year when you have a tight schedule or joining several small groups at the same time. If you set unrealistic and unattainable goals, you end up being overwhelmed and will ultimately give up.

Set Realistic Goals

Personal goals, then, need to be two things: first, correctly focused on areas of weakness you desire to strengthen; and second, attainable so they stretch you but don't overload you. Setting overambitious goals too early in the process will discourage you and possibly make you feel like giving up. Examples of realistic goals you could work on include getting up thirty minutes earlier than usual to spend time with God, going to bed earlier, reading through the New Testament, participating in one church small group, and finding a prayer partner to pray with regularly. These important steps will bring you one significant stage closer to your goal of developing your relationship with God.

Now it's your turn. The following chart provides an example of some realistic, small goals for spiritual growth. Look this over and then turn to Appendix A in the back of this book to create your own.

Monthly Training Program (sample)

February	Word & Prayer (Core)	Serve & Share (Arms)	Stretch (Legs)
Week 1	Read Matthew 1–7	Serve on ushering team	Wed. night small group
	Get up 6:30 A.M. for time with God	Tithe my income	Obey God's promptings
Week 2	Read Matthew 8–15	Serve on ushering team	Wed. night small group
	Get up 6:30 A.M. for time with God	Tithe my income	Obey God's promptings
Week 3	Read Matthew 16–22		Wed. night small group
	Get up 6:30 A.M. for time with God	Tithe my income	Mission trip preparation
Week 4	Read Matthew 23–28; Mark 1		Wed. night small group
	Get up 6:30 A.M. for time with God	Tithe my income	Mission trip preparation

10. Why is it important to set for yourself real, practical, spiritual goals?

_____

_____

11. What do you hope to achieve through a growth plan?

_____

_____

12. Read Philippians 3:14. What goal do you think the writer has in mind?

_____

_____

TRANSFORMATION FORMATION

Do not conform any longer to the pattern of this world, but be transformed by the renewing of your mind. Then you will be able to test and approve what God's will is—his good, pleasing and perfect will.
—Romans 12:2

We all struggle with our thought life: doubts, judgmental attitudes, bad moods, immoral thoughts, lies of the enemy about our identity, wrong understandings about God and His will, pride, and the list could go on. We all need help with our thought life, myself included, for as Proverbs 23:7 says, "For as he thinks in his heart, so is he" (NKJV). In other words, the person we are is determined by how we think. It's that simple.

Perhaps you're wondering, *How* does *transformation happen in our minds?* Good question.

Renew Your Mind: Meditate on God's Word

In Romans 12:2, the writer taught that transformation in our behavior happens through the *transformation of our minds*. And transformation of the mind happens through meditation on God's Word.

Don't misunderstand me. Meditation, as the Bible teaches, is not the emptying of one's mind, but rather the *engagement* of it. It's the deliberate act of weighing and reflecting on what a Bible passage says, something we often find in Scripture:

> Do not let this Book of the Law depart from your mouth; *meditate on it* day and night, so that you may be careful to do everything written in it. Then you will be prosperous and successful (Joshua 1:8, emphasis added).

> His delight is in the law of the Lord, and on his law he *meditates day and night*. He is like a tree planted by streams of water, which yields its fruit in season

and whose leaf does not wither. Whatever he does prospers (Psalm 1:2–3, emphasis added).

I have more insight than all my teachers, for *I meditate* on all your statutes (Psalm 119:99, emphasis added).

That's a lot of meditation, and a lot of benefit deriving from it. God's Word has the power to change wrong ideas, perspectives, ideologies, and the like, leading to permanent and positive change not just in our thinking, but in our whole life.

If you change how you think, you change how you live.

As you allow God's Word to transform your mind, another benefit is derived: you are suddenly able to understand confidently what God's will is for your life. Don't we all want more of that?

God's Word will nourish your heart and mind and, in turn, renovate your whole life. He wants to upgrade your life, for whenever we renovate and transform something, it's always for something better than before. I certainly wouldn't consider transforming my living room for uglier sofas or rugs. If I'm going to renew, I want something new and better. The same is true with us. God wants to transform us because He wants to give us something new and better: a better way of thinking, a better way of living, and a better understanding of His will.

Be careful what you put into your mind, for as with everything, we get out what we put in. The Bible clearly teaches what we should put into our minds:

> Fix your thoughts on what is true, and honorable, and right, and pure, and lovely, and admirable. Think about things that are excellent and worthy of praise" (Philippians 4:8, NLT).

> Those who live according to the sinful nature have their minds set on what that nature desires; but those who live in accordance with the Spirit have their minds set on what the Spirit desires (Romans 8:5).

Focus on the Light

Transformation doesn't happen overnight, but as we do our part, God will do His. Not only will God bring about genuine change in how we live, think, and speak, but, at the same time, we become prepared vessels for His great purposes:

> In a large house there are articles not only of gold and silver, but also of wood and clay; some are for noble purposes and some for ignoble. If a man cleanses himself from the latter, he will be an instrument for noble purposes, made holy, useful to the Master and prepared to do any good work. Flee the evil desires of youth, and pursue righteousness, faith, love and peace, along with those who call on the Lord out of a pure heart (2 Timothy 2:20–22).

Nutrition

It is supposed that all those vessels are useful to God, but in greatly varying degrees. As these verses imply, our pursuit of the things of God—righteousness, faith, love, and peace—will directly impact our usefulness to God. God wants us to pursue holiness, which happens through nourishing and feeding ourselves on the things of God. I love the insight Mike Bickle, director of International House of Prayer, offers in this quest for holiness:

> Many of the approaches to pursuing holiness have placed the emphasis of holy living on self-denial rather than fascination with God. It is biblical to call people to deny themselves of sinful lusts and pleasures. However, the best way to overcome darkness is not by focusing on the darkness of sin and trying to do our best to resist sin. The most practical and successful way to resist sin is to focus on *"the light of the knowledge of the glory of God in the face of Christ Jesus"* (2 Cor. 4:6) rather than the darkness of lust. No one seeks to remove darkness in a room by opening a window to throw out buckets full of darkness. The best way to remove darkness from a room is to simply turn on the light. We will not overcome the darkness of immorality, bitterness, and pride by focusing on it. We do not decrease the darkness in us by focusing on darkness. The way for darkness to decrease in us is for us to focus on increasing the amount of light we receive and enjoy. We overcome sin by actively encountering more of Jesus, not simply by resisting sin.[8]

It's a simple equation: the more of God we have in our hearts and minds, the less of our sinful nature. God has given us everything we need for that to happen: "His divine power has given us everything we need for life and godliness through our knowledge of him who called us by his own glory and goodness" (2 Peter 1:3). Nourish yourself therefore with the Word of God and pursue holiness, for then you will surely see the Lord (Hebrews 12:14).[9]

13. According to the passages in this section, what are some of the benefits of meditating on God's Word?

_____

_____

14. Read Hebrews 5:14. What does this verse teach about the capacity of solid food?

_____

_____

15. What are three practical things you can do to better nourish yourself spiritually?

_____

_____

Nutrition

APPLICATION QUESTIONS

Read through and prayerfully answer the following questions. Ask the Lord to guide you and speak to you.

1. Read 2 Corinthians 3:18. According to this verse, how is God transforming us?

   _____

   _____

2. What are some ways you can better train yourself to be godly?

   _____

   _____

3. Read John 4:31–34. What kind of food was Jesus referring to here? How does that apply to you?

   _____

   _____

4. What are some of the side effects you've experienced from a malnourished spiritual diet?

    _____

    _____

5. Is there any commitment in your life that is hindering you from growing in God? If so, what can you do to change that?

    _____

    _____

6. In your opinion, why is it important that we allow God to transform us?

    _____

    _____

7. What is one area God has spoken to you about through this chapter? How will you respond to Him?

    _____

    _____

Chapter 6

PERSEVERANCE

Perseverance must finish its work so that you may be mature and complete, not lacking anything.
—James 1:4

Have you ever heard of "hitting the wall" in a marathon? Every veteran runner I talked to prior to my decision to run my first marathon said the real halfway point isn't at thirteen miles, it's at twenty. They said somewhere around the twenty-mile mark, you're going to realize that's actually halfway. They were absolutely right.

Twenty miles into the marathon, my body said, *you're not going to run anymore,* and it started to shut down. I started feeling like my body was going into rigor mortis, and I began thinking, *I can't do this; it's really starting to hurt.* My mind was screaming at me, *Stop! Stop!* I had to make a willful, conscious choice to keep going. I had no energy. I had nothing except my willpower, which was fuelled by my faith.

As I looked forward to the end of the race, I wanted to know I had given it my all, that I had stayed faithful to it. I'm actually not a fit person by nature. Exercise has never been a part of my life. So that marathon was like a big dragon I had to slay.

During those final six miles, I was in pain, and I was angry. My friend Megan, who ran with me, was upbeat and trying to get me to keep going. I know I must have given her some looks as if to say, Shut up, Megan; leave me alone! I didn't want to run anymore. Everything I had was gone, except my faith. My phone had died and consequently I couldn't listen to my music. So I just started praying, reciting prayers I had learned.

When we finally reached the stadium at the end of the marathon, my body was broken and wracked with pain. Upon entering the stadium, I looked up and all these people I didn't know were clapping and shouting, "Good job! You did it!" It was an amazing feeling. Megan grabbed my hand and we ran across the finish line together. Then suddenly I saw the familiar faces of my friends, and they too were cheering and clapping, saying, "You did it! You can rest now. You finished the race." It was the closest thing I can imagine to how it will feel when we finish our race and make it to heaven.

Jacob

PURPOSES OF PERSEVERANCE

Therefore, since we are surrounded by such a great
cloud of witnesses, let us throw off everything that
hinders and the sin that so easily entangles, and let us
run with perseverance the race marked out for us.
—Hebrews 12:1

Successful athletes persevere in strenuous times to reach their longed-for goals. Whenever they face setbacks, injuries, problems with colleagues or coaches, illness, and the like, they understand that to win in their sport, they simply must persevere even when they don't feel like it. According to the United States Olympic Committee,

> Perseverance is staying focused on your goals and not giving up, even when your task is difficult. Real athletes train hard. They keep going, they press on and they persist in following their dreams. Sometimes they have to struggle against injuries or physical limitations. ... Perseverance is overcoming obstacles to reach your goals. ... Perseverance builds strength of character and confidence. It's a positive, winning attitude. Perseverance will make the difference between winning and losing on the field of play and in life.[1]

Perseverance is the final aspect of our training model, and there's much we can learn in this area from the professional world of sports. As spiritual athletes, we have desires we long to see fulfilled, prayers we hope to see answered, loved ones we desire to be saved, needs we want to be met. And we desire progress in our maturity and character. Therefore we too need to appreciate and understand the necessity to persevere and not give up when the going gets tough.

Toward that end we will consider two facets: first, the purpose that perseverance serves in our lives and, second, the tools that enable us to persevere.

Building Faith

> *According to your faith will it be done to you.*
> —Matthew 9:29

For numerous reasons, God allows us to go through seasons where we have to persevere to see prayers answered. Of course this is not always the case, but at some point in everyone's life, there will be occasions when this will happen. Undoubtedly, one of the main reasons God permits seasons of perseverance is to nurture faith within us.

One of the hardest parts of waiting for God is the inability to see and understand how God is working. In fact, and let's be honest, it can often appear that God isn't working at all. We neither see what He's doing in our lives nor understand His timing. It's incredibly hard to persevere when you see little, if any, change in your circumstances, especially when you've already been waiting for some time.

Essentially what is happening during this kind of season is the testing of your faith: Will God really answer my prayers? Why is He allowing this to take so long? Why can't I see Him doing anything? Yet despite how we feel and the many questions we ask God, Scripture says God is indeed working, though unseen.

This is precisely what living by faith is all about: living by the unseen. Look at how Hebrews 11:1 defines faith: "Now faith is being sure of what we hope for and certain *of what we do not see*" (emphasis added). Living by faith is more than living by what we see with our physical eyes. Living by faith, according to this verse, is living by what we do *not* yet see. It almost seems illogical, and in some ways it is, from a worldly point of view. Yet from a kingdom point of view, that, my friend, is the essence of living by faith. After all, it takes real faith to continue to trust God when you don't see things happening in the physical realm.

Think about some of the Biblical characters we've already looked at: David, who killed the giant Goliath with a pebble; Joshua and the Israelites, who saw the walls of Jericho fall by simply walking around them; Gideon and a few hundred other people, who God used to bring victory against a vast army. There's nothing logical about any of these situations. All God required from them was to place their confidence in Him in the midst of their impossible situations, and He did the rest.

God is answering your prayer for more faith. You desire that don't you? Greater faith is not a gift that is passively given; it's proactively sought after, and then given. As your faith is tested, it is stretched and through perseverance it grows. When your faith is put to the test, don't look upon your situation with worldly eyes. Look at your circumstances through eyes of faith, placing your confidence in God and His faithfulness. As you respond this way, God responds by providing a miracle, which, in turn, increases your faith even more.

Be sure of what you do not yet see. Perseverance brings its rewards.

Building Maturity

Consider it pure joy, my brothers, whenever you face trials of many kinds, because you know that the testing of your faith develops perseverance. Perseverance must finish its work so that you may be mature and complete. ... As you know, we consider blessed those who persevered.
—James 1:2–4; 5:11

This is probably the one purpose of perseverance you're most familiar with: the development of maturity. If you're anything like me, you've probably read these verses before and inwardly groaned. Yet these verses reveal that when our faith is being tested, there is a work going on: "Perseverance must finish its *work*." The work of perseverance is this: to develop maturity and completeness in your life.

We find God when we draw near in testing times.

It's precisely at such times of testing that God is doing some of His best work in us. God is always at work in our lives even though much of His work is usually unseen. The call to wait and persevere is never about the simple passing of time, for as you wait, your faith is strengthened and your experience of God is deepened. As James explains, God uses seasons of waiting to do a work *in* you as well as in

Perseverance

your circumstances: to deepen your relationship with Him, bringing you to maturity and completeness.

Many wonderful treasures can be found while waiting for God if you are willing to seek them out:

- a real experience of His power and faithfulness
- God speaking to you and guiding you
- divine resources to help and support you
- intimacy with God
- greater understanding of His love for you
- trustworthiness of His Word and promises
- learning how to really trust and love God
- the power and comfort of prayer
- the shaping of your heart in God's presence
- encouragement from other believers
- character development

These are some of the many blessings that are in store *if* you choose to persevere in this time of waiting. There is so much God wants you to know and experience about Him and His kingdom, but it can only happen when He has your full attention, and seasons of adversity have a way of creating that. Suffering has the ability to make us excellent listeners and learners if we are willing.

God's call for you to persevere has the power to deepen and develop your relationship with Him and mature you as an individual. This in turn will equip you to fulfill His purpose in your life. We all want to experience God and His power. We desire a better prayer life, to learn how to hear God's voice and feel His presence, and to discover His purpose and destiny for our lives. Beloved, God doesn't just download this information into us. It comes through drawing near to Him, and there's nothing like a season of waiting to motivate us to do that. As you give Him your full attention, He will speak to you, reveal His purposes to you, and do the all-important work of shaping and molding your heart and character: "Open your mouth wide, and I will fill it with good things" (Psalm 81:10, NLT).

1. Have there been moments in your life when God called you to persevere? What did you learn through those seasons?

    _____

    _____

2. How would you encourage a friend who is going through a test of faith?

    _____

    _____

3. Why do you think God sometimes seems silent before our prayers are answered?

    _____

    _____

POWER OF HIS PROMISES

*God is not a man, that he should lie, nor a son of
man, that he should change his mind. Does he speak
and then not act? Does he promise and not fulfill?*
—Numbers 23:19

Previously we looked at the purposes that perseverance can serve in our experience of God. We saw how God is always operating in our lives, using perseverance to do a very special work in us. Next I want to look at some of the specific tools that will enable us to persevere and not give up.

Without a doubt, the one thing that kept me going through tough seasons and gave me the will and hope to carry on was the truth of God's Word. I cannot overemphasize the importance of this. God's Word provides help in several crucial ways:

- It provides real strength and comfort.
- It reveals His will.
- It gives promises of His help and faithfulness.
- It offers guidance.
- It reveals the character and heart of God.

Confidence in God's Character

*The Lord, the Lord, the compassionate and
gracious God, slow to anger, abounding in love and
faithfulness, maintaining love to thousands.*
—Exodus 34:6–7

It is essential that we believe in the goodness of God. For some reason, one of the first things we question when our faith is being tested is God's character: Does God really keep His promises? Can I believe what He says? Does He really care for me?

A person's integrity is the one quality that enables us to believe and trust what he or she says, and this is a reality that carries over into our relationship with God. For instance, if we have no doubt of His goodness or His faithfulness, then we readily believe His Word. But if we're not sure of Him or the goodness of His plans and motives, that doubt will affect our confidence in His Word.

The wonderful news, as Numbers 23 declares, is that God never lies. He isn't fickle or unreliable, and because of His unchanging good character, His integrity, we can completely and utterly believe His promises. Believe me, there will be times in your life when that is all you have to hold on to. I can vividly remember deeply testing times in my own life, crying out to God in prayer, and clinging on to a particular promise or two. Because I had experienced His goodness and faithfulness earlier in my life, it was enough to give me the hope and strength I needed in His Word to persevere until His breakthrough came that time round.

You can trust what God's Word says.

There is so much unfaithfulness in our world today, but God is the One in whom you can have complete confidence. He is utterly faithful and trustworthy, and as you place your confidence in Him, you will experience the power of His promises and His amazing faithfulness.

God loves it when we trust in Him, though we often underestimate His goodness and kindness. However, as you make the important decision to believe what the Bible teaches and put all your hope in Him, He *will* come through for you. If you will persevere in faith, God will move in your situation in power in His perfect time. Once you've experienced God move like this, it will revolutionize your faith and relationship with Him.

Nourish Your Soul

> *The Lord is my shepherd; I have all that I need. He lets me rest in green meadows; he leads me beside peaceful streams. He renews my strength.*
> —Psalm 23:1–2, NLT

Too many of us are suffering from one particular ailment: starvation of the soul, a major cause of discouragement and weakness. No one is immune. We see even in Scripture how the best and most devoted men of God felt weak and subsequently questioned God's presence and faithfulness during difficult times:

> How long, O Lord? Will you forget me forever? How long will you hide your face from me? How long must I wrestle with my thoughts and everyday have sorrow in my heart? How long will my enemy triumph over me? (Psalm 13:1–2).

I say to God my Rock, "Why have you forgotten me? Why must I go about mourning, oppressed by the enemy?" My bones suffer mortal agony as my foes taunt me, saying to me all day long, "Where is your God?" (Psalm 42:9–10).

That's one exhausted and desperate man. Thankfully, there was hope for him, and there is hope for us. Although we, like David, may sometimes be tempted to think God has abandoned us and is not listening to our prayers, that's not the true picture. Despite what he felt, David always managed to seek God and thus find divine help in the midst of the most painful trial.

God will always provide what you need at that moment.

Beloved, we are never alone in our pain. We serve a good and faithful God who listens to the cries of His people and moves in response to help us. As the words of Psalm 23 promise, God renews our strength and restores our soul. As we turn to Him in prayer and cry out for His strength and help, He always answers. Perhaps God will bring a Scripture to mind or impress a statement or idea upon you. However He chooses to speak, God will always provide what you need at that exact moment. As the prophet Jeremiah knew, God will feed and nourish your soul, enabling you to persevere and carry on.

Blessed is the man who trusts in the Lord, whose confidence is in him. He will be like a tree planted by the water that sends out its roots by the stream. It does not fear when heat comes; its leaves are always green. It has no worries in a year of drought and never fails to bear fruit (Jeremiah 17:7–8).

These verses teach us a valuable lesson: *God gives us strength as we place our confidence in Him.* If you decide to renew your confidence in Him and His good character, you will find your soul divinely strengthened. God will feed and nourish you through His promises and give you what you need until the miracle comes. God is not far off as some suppose; He is actually very near: "The Lord is close to the brokenhearted and saves those who are crushed in spirit" (Psalm 34:18).

Like a shepherd, He leads us to peaceful and restful pastures to strengthen us again. In order to persevere through difficult seasons, it's important for you to understand that God really does know and care about what you're going through. God is not ignorant of your pain but, as the Bible reveals, He is aware of the turmoil His people suffer, and He moves to bring us through victoriously: "When you pass through the waters, I will be with you; and when you pass through the rivers, they will not sweep over you. When you walk through the fire, you will not be burned; the flames will not set you ablaze. For I am the Lord, your God" (Isaiah 43:2–3).

Things may get hot around us but we have no reason to fear, for God is with us and will miraculously bring us through the fire unscathed and unburned. He will do this as we, like King David, put our hope in Him:

Why are you downcast, O my soul? Why so disturbed within me? Put your hope in God, for I will yet praise Him, my Savior and my God (Psalm 42:11).

Dear friend, if you are passing through a difficult season, I pray the following Scriptures will encourage you and give you the confidence in God to press on until your answer comes.

- Delight yourself in the Lord and he will give you the desires of your heart (Psalm 37:4).
- Cast your cares on the Lord and He will sustain you; He will never let the righteous fall (Psalm 55:22).
- Trust in the Lord with all your heart and lean not on your own understanding; in all your ways acknowledge him, and he will make your paths straight (Proverbs 3:5–6).
- The Lord longs to be gracious to you; he rises to show you compassion. For the Lord is a God of justice. Blessed are all who wait for him! (Isaiah 30:18).
- Since ancient times no one has heard, no ear has perceived, no eye has seen any God besides you, who acts on behalf of those who wait for him. You come to the help of those who gladly do right (Isaiah 64:4–5).
- Therefore I tell you, do not worry about your life, what you will eat or drink; or about your body, what you will wear. Is not life more important than food,

and the body more important than clothes? ... But seek first [God's] kingdom and his righteousness, and all these things will be given to you as well (Matthew 6:25, 33).
- Therefore I tell you, whatever you ask for in prayer, believe that you have received it, and it will be yours (Mark 11:24).

4. How does God describe Himself in Exodus 34:6–7?

_____

_____

5. What is one promise of God's Word that has recently helped you?

_____

_____

6. Why do you think God's Word is so powerful and effective?

_____

_____

AVOIDING THE WALL

Why do you say, O Jacob, and complain, O Israel, "My way is hidden from the Lord; my cause is disregarded by my God"? Do you not know? Have you not heard? The Lord is the everlasting God, the Creator of the ends of the earth. He will not grow tired or weary, and his understanding no one can fathom. He gives strength to the weary and increases the power of the weak.
—Isaiah 40:27–29

As Jacob shared in the opening story of this chapter, those final six miles of his first marathon were by far the hardest. To him those six miles felt longer than the first twenty. Despite how he felt, he prayed to God and kept going despite what he was going through physically, emotionally, and mentally, until he crossed that finish line.

As believers, our whole experience of running with Christ is more akin to running a marathon than a sprint. For that reason, there may be moments when it feels as if we're hitting a wall; seasons that just seem too tough to carry on.

Perhaps God has asked you to wait upon Him for a particular answer to prayer and you've managed, through sweat and tears, to get to the "twenty-mile mark." Now though, you're completely exhausted and wonder just how you can keep going to the end. The exhaustion and discouragement we feel at such times have a way of making us vulnerable to doubt: Will God really answer my prayer? Why is it taking so long? Let's see what we can do to avoid hitting that wall.

Training Techniques

In Isaiah 40, God was speaking to people who were exhausted and on the verge of stopping and giving up. Their discouragement was so great that they had convinced themselves God had forgotten them and didn't even care about their situation. Doesn't sound so foreign, does it? The good news is, although we may see that wall approaching, it's not impossible to overcome or even avoid. Rick Morris writes,

> The wall is a somewhat intimidating term that is commonly used to describe the devastating feelings of fatigue and sometimes confusion that can occur in the final miles of a marathon. ... While the wall and the marathon distance are joined at the hip, that doesn't mean it can't be avoided or overcome. With proper training, intelligent race management and proper mental strategies you can avoid the marathon wall or at least minimize its impact on your race. ... Whether you want to avoid the wall completely or delay its effects until the finish line you can do that with proper training, race management and nutrition.[2]

Just as marathon runners turn to nutrition and training techniques to strengthen and equip them to beat the wall, we have tools that enable us to do the same. Spiritual fatigue is caused by malnourishment of the soul, as we've already seen. Proper nutrition on the Word of God will enable us to renew our confidence in God and His promises, which will in turn strengthen us. In other words, Scripture helps to realign our focus on God. Since we earlier looked at the vital role of spiritual nutrition, God's Word, let's think now about additional training guidelines that help us overcome that wall.

Realign Your Focus

Referring back to Isaiah 40, it's interesting to see how God addressed the problem of blurred perspectives among His people: "Do you not know? Have you not heard? The Lord is the everlasting God, the Creator of the ends of the earth. He will not grow tired or weary, and his understanding no one can fathom" (v. 28).

God's people had become overwhelmed with discouragement, so much so they questioned whether God really cared about what they were going through. In response, the Lord directed them to align their focus on Him and His power again. He reminded them that He was strong enough, powerful enough, and loving enough to help them around the wall they were experiencing.

The writers of the psalms were not immune from discouragement and the temptation to give up. Yet after they poured out their hearts to God in prayer, they refocused their concentration on God and His power and found faith and hope in Him again: "Then I thought, 'To this I will appeal: the years of the right hand of the Most High.' I will remember the deeds of the Lord; yes, I will remember your miracles of long ago" (Psalm 77:10–11).

Despite how this writer was feeling, he eventually realized he needed to fix his eyes on God once again and place his hope in His unfailing love. That takes a lot of courage and faith and is no easy decision. He understood that to see victory in the end, he simply had to realign his focus and believe God again.

We all sometimes forget how powerful and good God is. Our suffering looms so large and our needs feel so mountainous that doubt creeps in and we forget God is big and faithful enough to answer our prayers. Nothing is impossible to God, and focusing on God during moments of discouragement is essential to avoiding the wall.

God Your Superhero

The Bible clearly reveals that God delights in delivering His people from times of trouble:

> The Lord is my rock, my fortress and my deliverer; my God is my rock, in whom I take refuge. ... The cords of death entangled me; the torrents of destruction overwhelmed me. ... In my distress I called to the Lord; I cried to my God for help. From his temple he heard my voice; my cry came before him, into his ears. The earth trembled and quaked, and the foundations of the mountains shook; they trembled because he was angry. ... He parted the heavens and came down. ... He mounted the cherubim and flew; he soared on the wings of the wind. ... The Lord thundered from heaven; the voice of the Most High resounded. He shot his arrows and scattered the enemies, great bolts of lightning and routed them. ... He reached down from on high and took hold of me; he drew me out of deep waters. He rescued me

from my powerful enemy, from my foes, who were too strong for me (Psalm 18:2–17).

We all love a good sci-fi movie when the bad guy is destroyed by a strong superhero who has amazing superhuman powers. Yet God is far greater than any fictitious character we see on the screen. This particular psalm portrays God as thundering from the heavens, shooting His lightning arrows, and drawing His people out from the storms and dangers of life. If that isn't a picture of a superhero, I don't know what is! My friend, God is your personal Superhero, responding to the cries of the needy, using His might to meet your every need.

Analogy aside, God is incredibly powerful and loving when it comes to rescuing His children, whatever situation we may find ourselves in. God, who is on our side, loves to powerfully intervene and rescue us when we cry out to Him. What an amazing, all-powerful, and all-loving God we serve.

You are never alone. As you turn to God in prayer, He hears your cry and responds mightily to help you. God is more loving, powerful, and ready to help you than you think.

God's Power Manifest in Weakness

We've all been there: How long, O Lord? How long? Yes, there are moments when we feel so weak and we just don't know what to do. Despite how we feel, if we find the will to cry out to God, we can experience His help and power:

My grace is sufficient for you, for my power is made perfect in weakness. Therefore I will boast all the more gladly about my weaknesses, so that Christ's power may rest on me (2 Corinthians 12:9).

I can do everything through him who gives me strength (Philippians 4:13).

God never asks anyone to do anything in their strength alone. If that were the case, we wouldn't get very far at all. I know I wouldn't. Don't make the mistake of thinking you have to struggle through your current battle in your own strength. That is mistaken thinking, as is equating the power of God with merely finding the will to carry on.

The Bible teaches that the minute we acknowledge our true dependency on God and believe His promises, He is there to empower and strengthen us to do His will. I'm talking about experiencing the real and literal power of God that recharges and strengthens us.

One day recently I was feeling especially weary and discouraged. I've been waiting on God in an area of my life for around five or six years. I truly believe God will fulfill His promise to me, but sometimes discouragement tries to rear its ugly head. I felt so weak, even in my prayer time, but God in His kindness led me to a particular psalm. In that psalm the writer talked about worshiping the Lord, and I knew God was showing me the way out of my depression. Despite how I was feeling, later that day I made the deliberate faith choice to sing to and worship God for His goodness and faithfulness. You know what? That depression and discouragement completely disappeared! I felt renewed and myself again.

Faith choices release the power of God.

The Bible is replete with promises of the power and strength, protection and help of God in times of suffering and testing. If you are tempted to give up in your current situation, remember, God knows what you're going through and cares about your situation. He is your Superhero, and as you realign your focus on Him and worship Him in faith, He will give you the resources and strength you need to keep going until your breakthrough comes. Your felt weakness is an opportunity for you to experience God and His power like never before. As you acknowledge your weakness and in faith draw near to God, you will be strengthened by the power of the Holy Spirit. You don't have to be beaten by that wall.

7. Have you ever felt like you were "hitting the wall," spiritually speaking? How did you overcome it?

_____

_____

8. Read all of Psalm 18. How did God come to the rescue of David?

_____

_____

9. Read Isaiah 64:4. What does this verse promise God will do for the person who waits for Him?

_____

_____

COMPROMISES THAT CUT IN

You were running a good race. Who cut in on you and kept you from obeying the truth? That kind of persuasion does not come from the one who calls you. "A little yeast works through the whole batch of dough."
—Galatians 5:7–9

So far in this chapter we've looked at the purposes of God in perseverance and also the tools we can utilize to help us overcome. Next I want to consider how compromise and wrong influences can prevent us from growing in our faith. Let's look at the power that people, habits, or indulgences have over our lives and how they subsequently hinder our spiritual progress.

Do a Little Weeding

One of the greatest barriers to progressing and persevering in our faith is being drawn into compromise, which leads to being distracted off course. Compromise essentially is not being fully committed to one thing. It is a place that is "midway between two or more different things."[3]

Specific examples of compromise include:

- Yoking yourself together with a nonbeliever. This decision has the power to hold you back in your walk with God and His purpose for your life. This happens when you are encouraged to stop attending church as much as you normally would or pressured to engage in a physical relationship outside of marriage.
- Choosing a job promotion with a better salary and future prospects despite the fact it will mean more time at work and less with your family, God, and fellow Christians.
- Going along with underhand business practices at work, such as using office money without proper authorization, excessive drinking with business partners, visits to ungodly clubs, and so forth. If you do not honor God with your business ethics, how can God honor you?
- Busying yourself so much with personal commitments or clubs that you're not able to spend time with God and thus develop your relationship with Him.
- Agreeing to marry a nonbeliever, which leads to tensions in educating your children in the ways of God and conflict over values and priorities; also the inability to communicate about the things of God, attend church as a family, or be freely involved in church as you'd like.

Throw Off Wrong Influences

These examples of compromise are just some ways we can allow people or situations to interfere with or negatively influence our relationships with God. As Galatians 5:9 says, it takes just a little yeast to permeate a whole batch of dough, and, in much the same way, it takes just a little influence to do its negative work in our relationships with God.

We may not think at the time that one area of compromise makes much difference, but it does. Compromise is as powerful as yeast. Though at the time we may not recognize the danger of making unwise decisions, sooner or later we will most certainly feel their effects as the compromise hinders our spiritual progress.

We reap what we sow, and areas of compromise act like weeds in our lives, choking our faith and destroying the good progress we've already made. Allowing compromise to creep into your relationship with God, as many have painfully learned, never ends well. You simply cannot grow in God if you are compromising in an area of your life. The writer of Hebrews said, "Therefore, since we are surrounded by such a great cloud of witnesses, let us throw off everything that hinders and the sin that so easily entangles, and let us run with perseverance the race marked out for us. Let us fix our eyes on Jesus, the author and perfecter of our faith" (Hebrews 12:1–2).

I know this is not an easy topic, but, as these verses warn us, there are things that hinder our relationships with God, sins that entangle us. It can happen so easily and quickly before we've even realized what's going on. Satan knows it only takes one small area of compromise or disobedience to bring spiritual progress to a sharp halt. I've seen how quickly Satan uses any open door in my own life, and I see it in the lives of others I know who have stopped growing because of one area of compromise they have allowed.

Compromise not only holds us back from real spiritual growth, but it gives the devil a foothold in our lives (Ephesians 4:27), which I discussed in more depth in Chapter 1. Sin provides Satan the opportunity to trouble or oppress us in some way. Compromising in ways we know we shouldn't, telling ourselves, *God still loves me anyway. It'll be OK,* is spiritually irresponsible. The fact that God loves us is true, of course, but the danger of compromise is that it severely hinders your spiritual growth, power, and usefulness in His kingdom. There are too many believers today who do not understand this vital principle: *sin obstructs spiritual growth and gives the enemy a foothold in our lives.*

It takes just a little yeast to do its job in the whole loaf of bread, and, similarly, it just takes one issue to work its pervasive influence and effect in our lives. The Galatians had allowed themselves to be influenced by false teachers, but anything can have the effect of cutting in on your race with God.

Ask God to show you whether there is a relationship, commitment, or habit holding you back from growing spiritually. He will lovingly and gently bring it to mind, and when He does, I would encourage you to make the bold decision to cut it out of your life. I know it may sound a bit drastic, but as with any weed not dealt with, the roots will deepen and can ultimately stop you from walking with God altogether:

> And when people escape from the wickedness of the world by knowing our Lord and Savior Jesus Christ and then get tangled up and enslaved by sin again, they are worse off than before. It would be better if they had never known the way to righteousness than to know it and then reject the command they were given to live a holy life (2 Peter 2:20–21, NLT).

If you're in doubt about whether a particular influence is from God or not, then realize this: God will never put something or someone into your life that will hold you back from running your race well. Therefore, if something or someone is pulling you away from God, you can conclude it's not from Him. Remember, the work of the devil is to destroy your faith in God, so be alert and discerning of his tactics: "Be self-controlled and alert. Your enemy the devil prowls around like a roaring lion looking for someone to devour. Resist him, standing firm in the faith" (1 Peter 5:8–9).

God's will is that you run for Him and as you make wise and courageous choices to throw off all hindrances, you will grow in leaps and bounds and become the spiritual athlete you desire.

10. Is there something or someone hindering you from running your race? What or who is it, and what can you do to change that?

_____

_____

11. Read Luke 10:38–42. Martha allowed herself to be upset and distracted by many worries and chores. How did those distractions detract from her experience of listening to Jesus?

_____

_____

12. Now read Luke 6:46–49. Discuss the importance and relevance of what Jesus taught in these verses.

_____

_____

WHY YOU SHOULD NOT GIVE UP

Let us not become weary in doing good, for at the proper time we will reap a harvest if we do not give up.
—Galatians 6:9

At some point in your journey with God, there will be moments when you will be tempted to quit trusting in Him. There will be times when you will feel so weak and your situation so hard and impossible that you will seriously begin to question whether going God's way is worth it. If that is where you are right now, then this section is for you.

The Quality of God's Work

And we know that in all things God works
for the good of those who love him, who have
been called according to his purpose.
—Romans 8:28

Most of us are familiar with Romans 8:28, but some believers are not sure what it really means. Being asked to believe in the goodness of God during a season that seems anything but good takes a lot of courage and goodwill from the best of us. So what does this verse really mean? Rather, what does God's good work in our lives really look like? Is it enough?

It would be a beneficial exercise to evaluate the quality of God's good work by examining what the Gospels reveal about this subject. Throughout His ministry here on earth, Jesus Christ performed a lot of miracles, so many, in fact, that John wrote, "Jesus did many other things as well. If every one of them were written down, I suppose that even the whole world would not have room for the books that would be written" (John 21:25).

As the Gospel accounts teach, Jesus Christ set the oppressed free, forgave the sinner, restored sight to the blind, renewed lame feet, fed the hungry, taught the poor, welcomed children, healed the insane outcast, and loved the adulteress. I'm sure you'd agree that everything Christ did in people's lives was a wonderful outpouring of the love of God. Even the best unreligious person would have no problem admitting that the miracles Jesus performed were immensely good. That's not the problem. The issue many of us, both inside and outside the church, struggle with is understanding how God desires to work in our lives *today*.

Raise your opinion of God.

I believe the issue boils down to the essence of God's character: Does God actually *want* to heal or deliver or provide? Is He good enough? Did He cause all the trouble I'm experiencing? My friend, God is the author of good, not evil, in your life. He loves you so much more than you know and desires to give you many good things. Our God is a good and consistent God: "Don't be deceived, my dear brothers. Every good and perfect gift is from above, coming down from the Father of the heavenly lights, who does not change like shifting shadows" (James 1:16–17).

God does not change. Surely it follows, then, that the quality and attributes of His work have not changed. God is still working as He always has, bringing healing and hope into our lives. As Jesus once said, "The Spirit of the Lord is on me, because he has anointed me to preach good news to the poor. He has sent me to proclaim freedom for the prisoners and recovery of sight for the blind, to release the oppressed, to proclaim the year of the Lord's favor" (Luke 4:18–19).

The whole ministry of Jesus Christ centers on bringing life and healing in every way we could possible need it: spiritually, emotionally, and physically. This, my friend, is

God's will and intention for your life and the lives of your loved ones:

- to bring good news to the poor
- to bind up and heal the brokenhearted
- to proclaim freedom to the captive
- to provide release from chains of darkness
- to provide comfort in times of grief
- to exchange beauty for ashes
- to exchange joy for mourning
- to bring praise instead of despair[4]

In other words, Jesus provides everything you could possibly need to live life to the full (John 10:10). There is no sickness, addiction, oppression, or grief that God cannot bring you, or anyone you know, out of. Is God good? Yes, so very good. Are His plans for your life good? You can't even imagine how good: "Now all glory to God, who is able, through his mighty power at work within us, to accomplish infinitely more than we might ask or think" (Ephesians 3:20, NLT).

This is the heart of God and God's plans for you. You can trust Jesus, your good shepherd, with your life:

> "For I know the plans I have for you," declares the Lord, "plans to prosper you and not to harm you, plans to give you hope and a future. Then you will call upon me and come and pray to me, and I will listen to you. You will seek me and find me when

you seek me with all your heart. I will be found by you," declares the Lord (Jeremiah 29:11–14).

Good out of Bad

Not only is God working in qualitatively good ways in our lives, He is also able to bring tremendous good out of failure or tragedy in our lives. Such is the extent of His goodness.

In the following story, Canadian skier, Allison Forsyth, describes an injury she sustained just days before she was due to compete in the 2006 Olympics, and which prevented her from competing. Despite what seemed to be a personal failure, she came to experience great blessing as a result:

> About two weeks before the Olympic Games, my mom called me to let me know that her cancer was back. … I was concerned because with the stage 4 breast cancer that my mom had, any relapse could be fatal. … [Yet] my mom was coming to the Olympics in Torino to watch me compete. She said it was something she was going to do even if it was the last thing she ever did. But before that happened, I crashed and tore my left knee in the second training run of the Olympic downhill.
>
> From the moment I came out of surgery, I was healing, but my mom wasn't. The rapid decline in her motor skills and physical functioning made it clear to everyone that the cancer was rapidly attacking her system. … My mom would never have made it

to the race that day, and she probably would have died over there in Italy.

It's interesting how life presents us with challenges and basically taunts us into deciding what we are going to do with those challenges. Are we going to accept them and persevere, or are we going to let them crush us? This injury has been a challenge that I have chosen to persevere through. I have learned so much about myself, my life, and the people in it. I am committed to keep going until the Olympics in 2010.[5]

Although her injury forfeited her chance to compete in the 2006 Olympics, she came to understand that it served to extend her mother's life, giving Allison eight more precious months before her mother eventually passed away: "What happened to me at the Olympics has given me another eight months with my mom—time I would not trade for any gold medal in the world."[6]

You may not understand how God is working in your life right now, but how you respond to Him will determine the outcome. Will you decide to trust in Him and His goodness with all your heart? Can you dare to hope that God can bring great good even out of the worst of situations? Please understand that Satan, not God, is the author of evil. Yet when the tempests take their toll, God is right there ready to help, strengthen, and rescue you. If you will only choose to keep going and not give up hoping in God, you will experience God's goodness and power.

Joyce Meyer emphasizes the importance of a right attitude and perspective during seasons of waiting and persevering: "I have discovered that patience is not the ability to wait, but the ability to keep a good attitude while waiting."[7]

Know that persevering and waiting for God are never a waste of time, for God is working in you in so many ways, as we have looked at. Don't be tempted to blame God for your suffering, but understand that God can bring good out of anything, for nothing is impossible for Him, just as Joseph found: "As far as I am concerned, God turned into good what you meant for evil. He brought me to the high position I have today so I could save the lives of many people" (Genesis 50:20, NLT).

Joseph experienced betrayal and injustices at the hands of those around him, even his own family, yet God was able to turn around the evil he experienced for great good in his life. This was possible because he maintained his faith in God, understanding that God was not to blame for his suffering and would bring good out of it all. As you choose to place your hope and confidence in God's goodness for your present and your future, you too will see the goodness of God:

> Yet the Lord longs to be gracious to you; he rises to show you compassion. For the Lord is a God of justice. Blessed are all who wait for him! (Isaiah 30:18).

13. In your opinion, why is believing in God's goodness important for your future?

_____

_____

14. Why do you think relying on your own understanding of situations is dangerous spiritually?

_____

_____

15. Have you ever experienced God bringing good out of a difficult situation in your life? If so, how?

_____

_____

APPLICATION QUESTIONS

Read through and prayerfully answer the following questions. Ask the Lord to guide you and speak to you.

1. Read 2 Corinthians 4:7 and Ephesians 3:20. What do these verses teach us about God's power and resources for our lives?

2. How would you define "living by faith"? What's the hardest thing about that?

3. Why is it important that we stand on God's Word through seasons of adversity?

4. Read Isaiah 26:3–4. What do these verses promise to the person who trusts in God?

    _____

    _____

5. Do you believe God's goodness is enough to meet your needs? Why or why not?

    _____

    _____

6. Do you know of anyone who turned away from God after a difficult time? How could that have been avoided?

    _____

    _____

7. What is one area God has spoken to you about through this chapter? How will you respond to Him?

    _____

    _____

PART THREE

GO

Chapter 7

REACHING THE FINISH LINE

Let us fix our eyes on Jesus, the author and perfecter of our faith, who for the joy set before him endured the cross, scorning its shame, and sat down at the right hand of the throne of God.
—Hebrews 12:2

As I ran the final miles of the marathon, I remember thinking, *This has got to be over soon.* I was like a little engine: *Just keep running; just keep going.* Sure enough, we finally came around this corner and saw the Olympic Stadium welcoming us. What a magical moment. People were lined all along the sides and everyone was screaming.

We felt this surge of energy; a runner's "high." Then Jacob, my running partner, started crying. "It feels like we're running into heaven," he said. "The host of angels are cheering us on." I sensed the same thing; it really was the same imagery.

We entered the stadium and began running on the Olympic track. When we finally saw the finish line around the corner, we were both crying. Our friends were there, and I saw my husband, Collin, behind the finish line. One friend, John, had a camera and ran with us for the last little bit. Just seeing how excited he was for us to get there, and seeing everybody else at the finish line, was really amazing. As we ran down the home stretch, the memories flooded my mind—all the work, all the pain, all the days I chose to run and keep moving—and I knew it was completely worth it.

Jacob and I held hands, and when we crossed the finish line, I gave him the biggest, sweaty hug. We told each other, "I could never have done this without you. I'm so glad you are here with me." It was a pretty sentimental moment.

Later, Jacob and I reflected on how powerful that accomplishment was. Even just the experience of training every day taught us so much. We found that by being disciplined in that area of our lives brought discipline into other areas as well.

As I look back now, I'm so glad I pushed through the pain and that I had people who encouraged me along the way. It was so good that I would consider running another marathon!

I sometimes think about heaven, when I'm going to see my parents and all those other people who have been cheering me on. I think about Jesus waiting there for me at the finish line, scooping me up in His arms and telling me how proud He is of all the years I've run faithfully. That picture chokes me up every time I think about it.

Megan

AWARE OF EVIL SCHEMES

*When you forgive this man, I forgive him, too. And when
I forgive him (for whatever is to be forgiven), I do so with
Christ's authority for your benefit, so that Satan will not
outsmart us. For we are very familiar with his evil schemes.*
—2 Corinthians 2:10–11, NLT

Now that we've looked at the five areas of our training
model—*attitude, strength training, devotion, perseverance,*
and *nutrition*—I want to spend some time in this closing
chapter on the subject of spiritual warfare. As a disciple of
Christ, you need to know not only how to run your race
well, but you need to be equipped to withstand opposition
or challenges you may encounter along the way. What follows is teaching on how to stand firm in your faith, ensuring
that you overcome and eventually make it to your heavenly
finish line.

I don't want to sound overly spiritual, but it is Biblical
that we have an adversary who is seeking to bring destruc-
tive things into our lives to cause us to give up on our
faith journey. I don't like overemphasizing the work of
the enemy, for an unhealthy emphasis on the work of
Satan can cause us to take our eyes off Jesus. Even so, we
need to be aware of the fact that we have an adversary
and acquaint ourselves with his tactics. I have seen him
steal and destroy the faith of too many friends to not write
about this important topic.

Recognize Satan's Schemes

The devil's goal is quite simple: to destroy and spoil the good work of God in your life; to discourage you and defeat you thereby keeping you from fulfilling God's purposes and plans for you.

As the opening verses in this section show, Satan devises evil schemes to attack the children of God. The apostle Paul exposed one particular scheme of the enemy: unforgiveness toward a fellow brother. This is probably one of the most effective tactics of the enemy, for it is often successful in bringing division and strife among God's people, destroying the faith of many.

Beloved, Satan and his evil cohorts plan and scheme against the children of God, and we cannot afford to be ignorant of this fact. Time and time again, I've seen believers (including me) struggle with an issue, not realizing what's going on in the heavenly realms. This happens far too easily. What are some of the schemes the enemy uses against God's people? See if you recognize any of these:

- unwarranted opposition, which seemingly comes out of nowhere, from someone
- nightmares
- overbearing fear or condemnation
- immoral thoughts or desires you know are not your own
- feelings of oppression or heaviness
- depression
- experience of pain or illness before a ministry event
- feelings of hatred or bitterness toward someone

- blatant, practical attacks (unusual practical occurrences in your environment)

These are just some of the more common ways the enemy attacks the people of God. In fact, as we saw in Chapter 1, we give the devil a foothold or opportunity to bother us whenever we sin. Whatever form it takes, we can identify three common themes, which we shall now look at.

Your Relationship with God

The enemy uses a number of schemes to try to keep us from drawing near to God. One method is by convincing us of a lie about God's good character, and another is by filling us with fear. We'll look at a few examples that illustrate these.

A dear sister in Christ, let's call her Julia, recently told me about an experience she had in her home that left her feeling afraid and riddled with guilt. Julia is a fairly new believer who is earnestly seeking God. She is a victim of an abusive family background, but she has made great strides over the past few years and I have seen God bring healing into her life.

One evening, an object in her bedroom fell off a shelf and knocked over a small statue of a cross on another shelf. Later, her Bible opened to a page that talked about darkness soon coming. She was filled with fear and believed God was telling her that He was going to punish her. She tried to figure out why God was going to do this, and thought it was because she was not praying enough. That left her riddled with guilt. She genuinely thought this was the work of God! I explained to her that God doesn't work in such ways and that the guilt, condemnation, and fear she was experiencing were confirmation of that.

If you are unsure whether or not something you are experiencing is from God, look at the fruit. Does it draw you closer to God and the knowledge of His love for you, or does it drive you away from Him? Does it bring peace and joy only God can bring, or does it cause you to feel overwhelmed with fear or guilt? Compare your experience with what the Bible teaches about God's character and will: God is love and is slow to anger; He is patient, merciful, and kind.

Julia's experience was anything but good, and her lack of knowledge about God's good character caused her to become fearful. For a moment, the devil was able to deceive her, destroying her much-needed confidence and safety in her relationship with God.

Another example of a very blatant spiritual attack is one I personally experienced several years ago. I had just finished teaching my university class. It was about midday on a beautiful sunny day, and I got into my car to go home. As I closed the door, suddenly I heard a very loud noise, as if some large person or animal was on top of my car, wildly scraping each side, left and then right, over and over again. It was so loud and fast, it was obviously not human, and I immediately recognized it was the enemy's intention to frighten me. However, to my own amazement, I wasn't afraid. In fact, I laughed because I felt honored that I must have been doing something right to receive such an obvious attack. I simply drove home (keeping my hands firmly on the steering wheel, of course).

Whether they are obvious practical attacks, daily difficulties designed to frighten and discourage us from running after God, or simple lies about the character and work of God, Satan's tactics haven't changed much from the Garden of Eden. He is still using deception and lies to try to separate us from a real relationship with God. If he can convince you that God is to blame for some tragedy or difficulty in your life and thus cause you to stop drawing near to God, then he is achieving his goal. Please be aware of his schemes.

Your Relationship with Others

Our adversary hates unity and peace among God's people. He knows that when God's people are living in love, faith, and holiness, they are a mighty force to be reckoned with.

A church I was very familiar with many years ago was making tremendous progress in reaching out to the local community. The preaching was greatly anointed and God started bringing young people to faith, resulting in a flourishing youth ministry.

After a number of years, it became known that the pastor of this church, who was in his fifties, was having a secret relationship with a young girl in high school. When word got out, it devastated her family and caused great rifts in the rest of the church. Eventually, the church split into three, and a number of people lost their faith in God, blaming Him for allowing this to happen. The reputation of God and Christians in the local community was totally destroyed.

Sadly, this is not an uncommon story, and it's heart-breaking to see Satan successful in his schemes. Whether his plans involve individuals, families, or churches, our adversary is working to divide and destroy, and we need to be alert to his schemes.

Your Relationship with Yourself

Another way the enemy works is to keep you from realizing your true identity in Christ. One of his most effective strategies is to keep you out of the Word of God so you cannot discover the truth of who you are in Christ. He knows it takes only a little bit of compromise or guilt to do its work in the heart of a believer, so he will introduce those thoughts into your mind and heart to stop you from drawing near to God and immersing yourself in the Bible. When you as a child of God remain ignorant of God's Word, the enemy can convince you of any kind of lie, including these:

- God doesn't really have a purpose for your life.
- God doesn't love you.
- You are not important to God.
- You are not really saved.
- Your sins are not forgiven.
- God is punishing you.
- You are not good enough to read the Bible.

These are all lies of the enemy, yet it's surprising how effective they are. I remember one woman telling a brand new believer that she wasn't worthy to read the Bible because she knew nothing about it. She was told that to start reading the Bible with her level of ignorance as a new Christian would be dishonoring to God. I couldn't believe my ears when I heard this. This lie of the enemy kept this dear new believer from the Bible for many months before someone encouraged her to start reading it to learn about God.

Don't be unaware of the schemes of our adversary. Go back to the chart in Chapter 2 and remind yourself of the truths of God's Word in the face of these lies. Don't be afraid of the adversary, for you are on the winning side. Remember, Satan is already a defeated foe: "You, dear children, are from God and have overcome them, because the one who is in you is greater than the one who is in the world" (1 John 4:4).

You have God's power and presence living in you so you have no need to be afraid.

1. Have you ever experienced what you thought could have been spiritual warfare? What happened?

_____

_____

2. Read 1 Chronicles 21:1–8. What was the intention of Satan in this particular instance?

_____

_____

3. Now read Job 1:1–22. What do you learn about Satan's
    evil plan and intention in Job's life?

_____

_____

WEAPONS OF WARFARE

*[Jesus] replied, "I saw Satan fall like lightning from
heaven. I have given you authority to trample on
snakes and scorpions and to overcome all the power
of the enemy; nothing will harm you. However,
do not rejoice that the spirits submit to you, but
rejoice that your names are written in heaven."*
—Luke 10:18–20

One of the most important truths we need to be aware of
in spiritual warfare is that Satan is *not* an equal opponent
with God. Indeed, the Bible clearly teaches that Satan is a
defeated foe because of what Jesus accomplished through
the work of the cross:

> "Now is my soul troubled. And what shall I say?
> 'Father, save me from this hour?' But for this purpose
> I have come to this hour. Father, glorify your name."
> Then a voice came from heaven: "I have glorified
> it, and I will glorify it again." The crowd that stood
> there and heard it said that it had thundered. Others

said, "An angel has spoken to him." Jesus answered, "This voice has come for your sake, not mine. Now is the judgment of this world; now will the ruler of this world be cast out. And I, when I am lifted up from the earth, will draw all people to myself." He said this to show by what kind of death he was going to die (John 12:27–33, ESV).

Jesus was talking within the context of going to the cross. He explained what His sacrifice was going to achieve in terms of victory over the devil: the ruler of this world, Satan, was going to be cast out. Through His sacrifice on the cross, Jesus triumphed over the power of Satan, breaking his rule over the earth:

> And having disarmed the powers and authorities, he made a public spectacle of them, triumphing over them by the cross (Colossians 2:15).

> The reason the Son of God appeared was to destroy the devil's work (1 John 3:8).

At the cross, Satan's rule and power were defeated. This means you have no reason to be afraid of the work of the enemy. As Ron Phillips writes,

> Satan is a defeated foe because of the work of Christ on the cross, but he is also a formidable foe. Our struggle with him is likened to the famous battle

of New Orleans during the War of 1812. General Andrew Jackson commanded this greatest battle of the war after the papers of treaty had already been signed! Word had not reached them of these events.

We too fight in a battle that has already been decided. Jesus forever sealed the fate of the host of demonic forces and Satan himself when He died on the cross. Yet Satan still "walks about like a roaring lion, seeking whom he may devour" (1 Pet. 5:8).[1]

This lion may have a loud roar, but he is already conquered, since his power was defeated through the work of Jesus Christ on the cross and through His resurrection. You, my friend, are on the winning side.

Put on Your Full Armor

With that understanding in place, how then do we stand firm in our faith when we experience seasons of attack? Thankfully, the Bible answers this question for us:

> Finally, be strong in the Lord and in his mighty power. Put on the full armor of God so that you can take your stand against the devil's schemes. For our struggle is not against flesh and blood, but against the rulers, against the authorities, against the powers of this dark world and against the spiritual forces of evil in the heavenly realms. Therefore put on the full armor of God, so that when the day of evil comes, you may be able to stand your ground, and after you

have done everything, to stand. Stand firm then, with the belt of truth buckled around your waist, with the breastplate of righteousness in place, and with your feet fitted with the readiness that comes from the gospel of peace. In addition to all this, take up the shield of faith, with which you can extinguish all the flaming arrows of the evil one. Take the helmet of salvation and the sword of the Spirit, which is the word of God. And pray in the Spirit on all occasions with all kinds of prayers and requests. With this in mind, be alert and always keep on praying for all the saints (Ephesians 6:10–18).

This passage teaches that God has provided us with weapons of warfare, which we need to take up and use. In summary, these weapons are truth, righteousness, the gospel, faith, knowledge of salvation, the Bible, and prayer.

I've witnessed some believers "pray on" the armor as if it were some kind of invisible defense shield. That's not the correct way to put on the armor. Instead, each of these weapons is meant to be exercised and put into practice in our lives: as we walk in the paths of faith, truth, and righteousness; as we place our confidence in the gospel and in our salvation; and as we apply God's Word and prayer in our lives. As we proactively do these things, then we are correctly putting on and using our armor. Examples of using the armor include:

- choosing a promise of Scripture to hold on to when feeling discouraged (*sword of the Spirit*)

- maintaining your faith and trust in God in the face of impossible-looking circumstances (*shield of faith*)
- choosing to walk in righteousness when experiencing peer pressure (*breastplate of righteousness*)

These are practical ways of using God's armor in the face of everyday warfare.

But it's not enough to use just some of these weapons. For example, just praying without meditating on God's Word will leave some of your defenses down. What good soldier would enter battle with a shield but no sword? Or a sword, but no shoes? It would be suicide.

If you desire to stand firm in your faith in the day of battle, you need to put on every piece of God's armor. It's not enough to cover your head and feet while leaving your body exposed. I'm sure you wouldn't go into battle like that, so why fail to put on the whole armor of God? It's only when you are fully covered that you are best able to resist and overcome the enemy: "Therefore put on the *full* armor of God" (v. 13).

4. Read Colossians 1:13. According to this verse, what spiritual transaction has taken place in our lives?

_____

_____

5. How would you describe taking up the "sword of the Spirit" (Ephesians 6:17)? Can you think of a personal practical example?

_____

_____

6. What do you think it means to "be alert," as Ephesians 6:18 talks about?

_____

_____

SOURCES OF CONFLICT

Submit yourselves, then, to God. Resist the devil, and he will flee from you.
—James 4:7

One reason some people struggle to overcome personal battles is that they are not submitting to God's will in their lives. According to our opening verse in this section, your ability to effectively resist the enemy is not simply about using weapons of warfare. It begins with your submission to God's will. Let me put it another way: you will only be able to effectively overcome the adversary's attacks if you are walking in obedience to God, thus preventing the enemy from gaining a foothold in your life. When you walk obediently and stand in your full armor while resisting your adversary, he will surely flee from you. That's God's promise.

Two Kinds of Battles

There are basically two kinds of battles we experience as believers:

1. *External battles:* These are practical occurrences that do not originate from ourselves and are not a direct result of our decisions and behavior. I mentioned earlier the examples of Julia and my experience in my car.

2. *Internal battles:* These are pretty much self-inflicted. In other words, they are the result of unwise decisions, relationships, or behavior that we are directly responsible for. Examples include addictions, disorders, confusion, instability, certain sicknesses, oppression, idolatry, and the like.

While it's easy to blame every difficulty on the work of the enemy, sometimes we encounter spiritual attack because we've left a door open for the enemy to come against us. Beloved, we cannot pray our way out of a situation we've behaved our way into. It doesn't happen like that. There are consequences to every decision and action we take, and we sometimes experience warfare because of our own doing.

I remember one vivid example of this in my own life. I was having a battle in a particular relationship. Although we had known each other for years, our relationship had made absolutely no progress no matter what I tried. This person's heart was closed to me although I had done nothing to warrant that. I just wanted to love and support her.

When I faced this person again, feelings of dread overcame me. I struggled with these heavy emotions for days, crying out to God for His help. Eventually God enabled me to realize I was harboring unforgiveness toward her for her indifference and unkindness all those years. Regardless of how she was treating me, I knew it was my responsibility to forgive her, even though it wouldn't bring about any change in the relationship. After all, she didn't even know I was going through the process of forgiving her. I made the decision before God, forgiving her for the hurt I felt. Immediately I felt the burden lift, and I was amazed as God took that overwhelming dread away. When I later saw her, I felt so free.

This is one simple example of how our own decisions or behavior can open the door to spiritual attack and oppression from the enemy. If you are undergoing what you think is some kind of spiritual warfare, come to God in prayer and ask Him whether there is anything you need to do to see your breakthrough.

Setting the Prisoner Free

> *He has sent me to bind up the brokenhearted,*
> *to proclaim freedom for the captives and*
> *release from darkness for the prisoners.*
> —Isaiah 61:1

God is without a doubt in the business of healing broken lives today all over the world. Yet the key to receiving freedom from internal battles, addictions, oppression, or sicknesses that have a spiritual origin is our submission to God—that is, our willingness to change and go God's way.

I find it interesting that if you speak to people who have had a long-term addiction, for example, most will tell you they have a problem. Yet despite their humble understanding, the issue lies with their willingness to change and let go of it.

I'm talking about repentance. Beloved, God can set people free from any of these disorders only if they are willing to change. You don't have to try to overcome the problem yourself. After all, you can't; that's why the problem has lasted so long. Setting someone free is God's work. What you need to do is sincerely repent, seek God's forgiveness through faith in Jesus Christ, and then God will do two great things for you: forgive you completely, giving you a brand new start, and set you free from the actual problem. That's what Isaiah 61 is talking about. As you make the brave decision to submit to God and start doing things His way, I promise you will be amazed at what God can do in your life.

It's never too late. I know true stories about people who, at their worst moments, cried out to God in repentance and the Spirit of God dramatically healed and delivered them, right then, right there. No one is ever too far gone. You cannot even imagine the beautiful work God can do with a surrendered life. It's His specialty.[2]

7. Is there something in your life you long for God to set you free from? What is it? How do you think God wants you to respond to see freedom?

_____

_____

8. Have you ever experienced God setting you free from a personal battle? Please share that.

_____

_____

9. Why do you think God's power is released *following* repentance?

_____

_____

OBTAINING VICTORY ON THE BATTLEFIELD

For though we live in the world, we do not wage war as the world does. The weapons we fight with are not the weapons of the world. On the contrary, they have divine power to demolish strongholds.
—2 Corinthians 10:3–4

So far in this chapter we've considered the different kinds of spiritual battles that can go on in our lives and how to use the weapons of warfare God has provided for us to walk into victory. Next we're going to look at how God wants us to respond in the face of external battles.

Not Your Battle

One common mistake we can make when faced with a battle is carrying the burden of the battle upon ourselves. We forget the important truth that the battle does not belong to us, but to God. He is sovereign over every battle in our lives and fights on our behalf.

The Biblical story of King Jehoshaphat and the time he was about to face defeat from opposing forces illustrates well both the response God desires from us and His counter-response:

> Some men came and told Jehoshaphat, "A vast army is coming against you from Edom, from the other side of the Sea." ... Alarmed, Jehoshaphat resolved to inquire of the Lord, and he proclaimed a fast for all Judah. The people of Judah came together to seek help from the Lord. ...
>
> Then Jehoshaphat stood up in the assembly of Judah and Jerusalem at the temple of the Lord ... and said: ...
>
> "O our God, will you not judge them? For we have no power to face this vast army that is attacking us. We do not know what to do, but our eyes are upon you."

All the men of Judah, with their wives and children and little ones, stood there before the Lord.

Then the Spirit of the Lord came upon Jahaziel son of Zechariah. ... He said, "Listen, King Jehoshaphat and all who live in Judah and Jerusalem! This is what the Lord says to you: 'Do not be afraid or discouraged because of this vast army. For the battle is not yours, but God's. Tomorrow march down against them. They will be climbing up by the Pass of Ziz, and you will find them at the end of the gorge in the Desert of Jeruel. You will not have to fight this battle. Take up your positions; stand firm and see the deliverance the Lord will give you'" (2 Chronicles 20:2–17).

Can you imagine the scene? A vast army comprising of three people groups were coming against God's people. Another David and Goliath scenario, it would seem. So what can we learn from their situation?

First, whenever faced with a personal battle, the right reaction is always to turn to the Lord for help as our first, not last, resort. King Jehoshaphat didn't bother mustering his army together or sharpening their swords, as would have been the norm. The only thing he did was turn to God in utter dependence and trust in Him.

Second, God taught Jehoshaphat the correct perspective: it was not his battle to fight, but God's. He and the people wouldn't have to lift a sword. They just needed to take God at His Word and stand firm in their faith in God. Here's what happened the following day:

After consulting the people, Jehoshaphat appointed men to sing to the Lord and to praise him for the splendor of his holiness as they went out at the head of the army, saying:

"Give thanks to the Lord,

for his love endures forever."

As they began to sing and praise, the Lord set ambushes against the men of Ammon and Moab and Mount Seir who were invading Judah, and they were defeated. …

When the men of Judah came to the place that overlooks the desert and looked toward the vast army, they saw only dead bodies lying on the ground; no one had escaped (vv. 21–24).

It's no coincidence that as King Jehoshaphat and his men praised and worshiped God in the front lines of battle, God set ambushes and brought about the victory. When we worship God in the heat of battle, trusting Him to intervene on our behalf and giving Him thanks, as illogical as it seems, we are essentially saying to God, "I believe you love me and will help and rescue me," and God loves that kind of faith. Not only that, it releases the power of God.

Friend, that battle you're going through right now is not even your battle to contest. It is God's and He wants to fight it for you. He does require a couple things from you though: your confidence in His love and dependence upon Him. Give Him the battle and worship Him in the face of it, and you will see what God will do on your behalf.

Trust God's Righteous Rule

Should you experience an external spiritual attack, it is essential you remember this one fact: God is sovereign and reigning over the situation. When we're experiencing spiritual warfare, it's easy to become excessively focused on what we're experiencing and, in turn, lose sight of God. Beloved, please remember, when you're in the midst of a battle or conflict of some kind, look to God and place your confidence in His righteous rule. Your confidence in God is a weapon the enemy cannot stand up against.

Consider this verse: "I trust in the Lord for protection. So why do you say to me, 'Fly like a bird to the mountains for safety!'?" (Psalm 11:1, NLT). David was once again being threatened by his enemies, who seemed to have the upper hand. Yet despite the threatening situation, David chose to place his confidence in God's righteous rule and vindication in this situation, believing God would bring about justice and deliverance in the end. When his enemies thought he should flee from them, he refused to give in to such despairing thoughts and instead remembered God's sovereignty over his situation, even over his enemies. He believed God would protect him from the threats of his enemies, and He did.

I learned the power of confidence in God's righteous rule during a recent battle. Out of nowhere I started to receive strong opposition from someone near me, the reason for which I couldn't fathom. It felt like a huge mountain, and I felt oppressed and alone. I cried out to God to help me and He led me to Psalm 11:1, which brought great comfort and strength. I learned that God is ruling and He will protect us.

If you are experiencing an overwhelming situation, take heart from those words penned by David. Know that you don't need to despair and run away, because God is ruling in your life and will intervene for you. He sees what is going on and will protect you and turn the situation around as you trust in Him. Place your confidence in His ability to rescue you, trust Him for your protection, and you will overcome the taunts and schemes of the enemy.

Prayer Support

Another powerful weapon that brings about victory is the prayer support of godly friends. When I was going through the opposition I mentioned, I was so desperate that I asked a couple friends whose wisdom and maturity I trusted to pray for me. I shared the problem, and simply asked for their prayer. God quickly answered. The following day at a certain time, I suddenly became aware that the oppression I had been feeling the previous week had suddenly lifted, for God had taken it away. I was relieved and thankful. I rejoiced knowing that this breakthrough was due to the prayers of my friends.

Understand that God is sovereign over the spiritual battle going on around you and has provided the means for you to see victory. You don't need to feel defeated or alone. Nor do you need to run away. Instead, put on the whole armor of God, turn to God, worship Him, place your confidence in His righteous rule, and seek the prayer support of friends. As you make God your protection, you will see Him defend you and bring about victory.

Every battle and race in life comes to an end. Victory is near. The answers to your prayers are coming, the breakthrough is in sight, so don't give up. Place your hope in God's goodness and in His Word, and you will see God slay your Goliath.

10. Have you ever experienced some kind of opposition that seemed to spring out of nowhere? If yes, please share.

_____

_____

11. What did you especially like from the story of King Jehoshaphat's victory?

_____

_____

12. Read 2 Corinthians 10:3–4. What do we learn about our spiritual weapons in these verses?

_____

_____

WORK OUT YOUR SALVATION

If anyone competes as an athlete, he does not receive the victor's crown unless he competes according to the rules.
—2 Timothy 2:5

We have finally come to the end of our journey together, so a big "well done" to you! You have persevered through this study and I'm very proud of you. I pray this book has been useful to you and that you have discovered how you can mature even further as a disciple of Christ and obtain the kind of relationship with God you've always wanted.

To close, I want to look at another subject that isn't easy for us but that we need to examine together nonetheless. I'm talking about the need to work out your salvation with fear and trembling.

When I read through the New Testament, I notice numerous calls to persevere and not fall away in my faith. As I've mentioned before, I've seen dear friends, who were once sincerely walking with God, fall away from Him. Perhaps you have too. People do not choose to walk away from God for no reason. Often it's because of some injustice or unfair treatment they experienced; sometimes it sadly comes about at the hands of other Christians. A lack of proper understanding of God's ways and the schemes of the evil one leads people to place the blame at God's door when such difficulties arise.

Dear friend, things will happen in your life that will tempt you to go down the same road. That is why several New Testament writers often urged their readers to not turn away from the living God. Consider the following verses penned by the writer of Hebrews:

> It is impossible for those who have once been enlightened, who have tasted the heavenly gift, who have shared in the Holy Spirit, who have tasted the goodness of the word of God and the powers of the coming age, if they fall away, to be brought back to repentance, because to their loss they are crucifying the Son of God all over again and subjecting him to public disgrace.
>
> Land that drinks in the rain often falling on it and that produces a crop useful to those for whom it is farmed receives the blessing of God. But land that produces thorns and thistles is worthless and is in danger of being cursed. In the end it will be burned.
>
> Even though we speak like this, dear friends, we are confident of better things in your case—things that accompany salvation (Hebrews 6:4–9).

Tough words. The writer is clearly talking about people who were once walking with God and even experienced the power of God, His Word, and His Holy Spirit, and yet they eventually fell away. It seems impossible doesn't it? But it can happen. So what can we do to prevent that from happening in our own lives?

Authentic Faith

Salvation is not a gift you receive once and therefore attain no matter how you live your life. The Bible clearly teaches that anyone who thinks they can call Jesus "Lord" and then live exactly as they please, doing what they want with what God has entrusted to them, are deceiving themselves:

> The Lord answered, "Who then is the faithful and wise manager, whom the master puts in charge of his servants to give them their food allowance at the proper time? It will be good for that servant whom the master finds doing so when he returns. I tell you the truth, he will put him in charge of all his possessions. But suppose the servant says to himself, 'My master is taking a long time in coming,' and he then begins to beat the menservants and maidservants and to eat and drink and get drunk. The master of that servant will come on a day when he does not expect him and at an hour he is not aware of. He will cut him to pieces and assign him a place with the unbelievers" (Luke 12:42–46).

Both Hebrews and Luke are addressed to believers, and both passages talk about what God will do to the person who is unfaithful toward Him in their lives: they will be punished as unbelievers.

Do not take salvation for granted. Whether we are truly saved will evidence itself through the genuineness of our professed faith and subsequent life path. A one-time profession is not enough. Only those who persist and show their faith through their good deeds and fruit will be saved. In other words, we need to put into action God's saving work in our lives and show we truly have repented: "Prove by the way you live that you have repented of your sins and turned to God" (Matthew 3:8, NLT).

Too many people attend church services each weekend and live as they please the rest of the week, yet believe they are saved. There is little evidence of real repentance in their lives, however. They think their belief in the existence of God is enough to be saved. They are sadly mistaken. James clarifies it well:

> What good is it, my brothers, if a man claims to have faith but has no deeds? Can such faith save him? Suppose a brother or sister is without clothes and daily food. If one of you says to him, "Go, I wish you well; keep warm and fed," but does nothing about his physical needs, what good is it? In the same way, faith by itself, if it is not accompanied by action, is dead.
>
> But someone will say, "You have faith; I have deeds."
>
> Show me your faith without deeds, and I will show you my faith by what I do. You believe that there is one God. Good! Even the demons believe that—and shudder (James 2:14–19).

James explains there are two kinds of faith: a living faith and a dead faith. Dead faith, which bears no fruit, will not save you in the end. Even demons have that kind of faith, and they are most certainly not saved.

The question you need to ask yourself is what kind of faith you have. Is it or is it not a real and living faith, evidencing itself by your good deeds? The genuineness of your confession will be seen by how you live: "Therefore, my dear friends, as you have always obeyed … continue to work out your salvation with fear and trembling" (Philippians 2:12).

13. Describe in your own words the kind of faith God is looking for in our lives.

_____

_____

14. Why do you think the Bible emphasizes evidence of genuine faith?

_____

_____

15. Why is a correct perspective of God's character so essential for us?

_____

_____

APPLICATION QUESTIONS

Read through and prayerfully answer the following questions. Ask the Lord to guide you and speak to you.

1. Would you say the authenticity of your faith and repentance is distinguishable in how you live?

   _____

   _____

2. What is one weapon of warfare you need to learn how to better use?

   _____

   _____

3. What can happen in our lives if we do not submit ourselves in obedience to God?

   _____

   _____

4. What is the role of prayer in the area of spiritual warfare?

_____

_____

5. Do you know someone who is going through a season of possible spiritual attack? What can you do to help and support him or her at this time?

_____

_____

6. What is one thing you can do this week to run your race better?

_____

_____

7. What is one area God has spoken to you about through this chapter? How will you respond to Him?

_____

_____

Epilogue

. . . .

RUN YOUR RACE WELL

I consider my life worth nothing to me, if only I may finish the race and complete the task the Lord Jesus has given me—the task of testifying to the gospel of God's grace.
—Acts 20:24

God has great plans for your life if you are willing to completely consecrate yourself to Him and His purposes, if you are willing to live a life of obedience:

> Obedience to God's will is the secret of spiritual knowledge and insight. It is not willingness to know, but willingness to do (obey) God's will that brings enlightenment and certainty regarding spiritual truth. ...
>
> Pure in speech. Pure in body. Pure in habits. ... The temptation of impurity cannot be fought on one battlefield alone. It is intimately connected with lack of discipline, laziness, self-indulgence in food, sleep,

and habits. If you let the body master you in some things, it will tend to be master in everything. *Self-discipline is essential in the Christian life.*"[1]

Eric Liddell knew what he was talking about when he penned these words, for as we know, he was a champion in both the physical and spiritual realms. He had learned well the need for discipline to reap the desired rewards. It is no different for us.

Jesus once said, "My food ... is to do the will of him who sent me and to finish his work" (John 4:34). Can you say the same? Beloved, only the work of God can truly satisfy.

God's earnest desire for you, my friend, is that you live your life for Him and His will and kingdom purposes. He wants all footholds and obstacles to be cleared from your path, so you may run with a fully surrendered heart and mind. God intends for you to become a spiritual athlete who is vigilantly and wisely running with Him; running with your eyes fixed on Jesus and experiencing God like you've never done before.

Are you ready to become that empowered athlete and have that kind of relationship with God? Are you willing to go the distance with your Savior and invest in all five areas: *attitude, strength training, devotion, perseverance,* and *nutrition*? It is not enough to admire Christ; it is not enough to believe in Him; only athletes who give it their all are worthy:

> We ask God to give you complete knowledge of his will and to give you spiritual wisdom and understanding. Then the way you live will always honor and

please the Lord, and your lives will produce every kind of good fruit. All the while, you will grow as you learn to know God better and better (Colossians 1:9—10, NLT).

Run in such a way as to get the prize (1 Corinthians 9:24) and you will find yourself on the greatest adventure of your life!

CLOSING PRAYER

Dear God, help me become the spiritual athlete You can be proud of. Enable me to grow in my attitude, strength training, devotion, perseverance, and nutrition so I can live a life pleasing to You. I want to know You more and more and to love and trust You in all areas of my life. Thank You that You want to use me to bless others. Help me, Lord, to learn how to truly live by Your Spirit and run my race as You desire. In Jesus' name I pray, amen.

Appendix

MONTHLY TRAINING PROGRAM

$\int$ pend some time to tailor your own spiritual training program to stimulate real spiritual growth in your life.

Month:	Word & Prayer (Core)	Serve & Share (Arms)	Stretch (Legs)
Week 1			

Week 2			
Week 3			
Week 4			

For more resources and information, including free videos, Bible reading assistance, and help for small group leaders, visit the author's website at www.realate.org/

ENDNOTES

CHAPTER 1

1   Terry Orlick, *In Pursuit of Excellence: How to Win in Sport and Life through Mental Training* (Illinois: Human Kinetics, 2008), 4.

2   J. Oswald Sanders, *Spiritual Discipleship: Principles of Following Christ for Every Believer* (Chicago: Moody Publishers, 1994), 93–94.

3   Cindy Jacobs, *Deliver Us from Evil* (California: Regal, 2001), 216.

4   John Bevere, *Enemy Access Denied: Slam the Devil's Door with One Simple Decision* (Florida, USA: Charisma House, 2006), xi.

5   If you feel you have more serious spiritual issues to deal with, including strongholds of the enemy, I recommend Neil T. Anderson's many excellent books, including the spiritual "house-cleaning" curriculum, *Steps to Freedom in Christ*.

6 Every Christian needs to be both baptized in water and baptized in the Holy Spirit to live the empowered life God desires for us. Please refer to Chapter 9 in *10 Steps to Knowing God* for more on this subject.

CHAPTER 2

1 Joyce Meyer, *Battlefield of the Mind: Winning the Battle in Your Mind* (New York: Faith Words, 1995), 27.

2 Some excellent books on this subject of renewed thinking are *Who I Am in Christ* by Neil T. Anderson and *Battlefield of the Mind* by Joyce Meyer.

3 Tom Doyle, *Dreams and Visions: Is Jesus Awakening the Muslim World?* (Nashville, Tennessee: Thomas Nelson, 2012), 3–4, 7.

4 John Dawson: *Taking Our Cities for God: How to Break Spiritual Strongholds* (Florida, USA: Charisma House, 2001), 34.

5 Roberts Liardon, *God's Generals: The Healing Evangelists* (New Kensington, PA: Whitaker House, 2011), 291.

6 Mark Vella, *Anatomy for Strength Training and Fitness Training for Women* (UK: New Holland, 2008), 15.

7 John Bevere, *Enemy Access Denied: Slam the Devil's Door with One Simple Decision* (Florida, USA: Charisma House, 2006), 106.

CHAPTER 3

1 Alan Keiran, *Take Charge of Your Destiny* (Shippensburg, PA: Destiny Image Publishers, 2008), 91.

2   Greg L. Hawkins, Cally Parkinson, *Move: What 1,000 Churches Reveal About Spiritual Growth* (Grand Rapids, USA: Zondervan, 2011), 18–19.

3   *Ibid.,* 9.

4   John W. Keddie, *Finish the Race* (Scotland, UK: Christian Focus, 2011), 47, 52.

5   You can be blessed from the materials about these great men and women of God on his website, www.godsgenerals .com.

6   Nick Vujicic, *Life without Limits* (New York: Doubleday Religion, 2010), 28.

7   Orlick, *In Pursuit of Excellence,* 32.

CHAPTER 4

1   Michael Lardon, *Finding Your Zone: Ten Core Lessons for Achieving Peak Performance in Sports and Life* (New York: Penguin, 2008), 19.

2   www.merriam-webster.com and www.thefreedictionary .com.

3   Lardon, *Finding Your Zone,* 75.

4   Orlick, *In Pursuit of Excellence,* 4.

5   *Ibid.,* 75.

6   Eric Liddell, *The Disciplines of the Christian Life* (Escondido, CA: eChristian Inc, 2011), 46.

7   Jim Loehr and Tony Schwartz, "The Making of a Corporate Athlete" (*Harvard Business Review,* January 2001), 122.

8   Liddell, *Disciplines of Christian Life*, 47.

9   www.sermonindex.net.

CHAPTER 5

1   Gabriel Sey, *Ultra Fit, Vol.22, No. 4, April 2012*, 46.

2   Kimberly Nunley, *Why I Am Losing My Muscles*, www.live strong.com, June 14, 2011.

3   I highly recommend using C. Peter Wagner's Spiritual Gift Assessment to discover the gifts God has entrusted to you. You can purchase this tool online at all good Christian bookstores. Read more on the gifts in Romans 12:4-8, 1 Corinthians 12, and 1 Corinthians 14.

4   Orlick, *In Pursuit of Excellence*, 34.

5   Chris Zaremba, "Nutrition Transformation" (*Ultra Fit, Vol.22, No.4, April 2012*), 73.

6   James E. Loehr, *The New Toughness Training for Sports: Mental, Emotional, and Physical Conditioning from One of the World's Premier Sports Psychologists* (New York: Penguin Putnam, 1995), 180–81.

7   *Ibid.*, 182.

8   Mike Bickle with Brian Kim, *7 Commitments of a Forerunner: A Sacred Charge to Press into God* (Kansas City, MO: Forerunner Publishing, 2009), 94–95.

9   For further help in this area of renewing the mind, I highly recommend *Battlefield of the Mind* by Joyce Meyer.

CHAPTER 6

1 www.teamusa.org.

2 Rick Morris, "The Marathon Wall: What It Is and How to Beat It," www.runningplanet.com.

3 World English Dictionary online.

4 Isaiah 61:1–3.

5 Orlick, *In Pursuit of Excellence*, 255–56.

6 *Ibid.*, 256.

7 Meyer: *Battlefield of Mind*, 223.

CHAPTER 7

1 Ron Phillips, *Everyone's Guide to Demons and Spiritual Warfare: Simple, Powerful Tools for Outmaneuvering Satan in Your Daily Life* (Florida: Charisma House, 2010), 43.

2 For more on this subject, I highly recommend the teaching of Neil T. Anderson: *The Steps to Freedom in Christ, The Bondage Breaker,* and *Freedom from Addiction.*

EPILOGUE

1 Liddell, *Disciplines of Christian Life*, 27, 70–71.

CPSIA information can be obtained at www.ICGtesting.com
Printed in the USA
BVOW03s1430240314

348598BV00001B/51/P